THE GAY WORLD

THE
GAY
WORLD

Male Homosexuality and the
Social Creation of Evil

by

MARTIN HOFFMAN

BASIC BOOKS, INC., PUBLISHERS

New York   London

Second Printing

© 1968 by Basic Books, Inc.
Library of Congress Catalog Card Number: 68–54131
Manufactured in the United States of America
Designed by Loretta Li

For Beatrice

But people can't, unhappily, invent their mooring posts, their lovers and their friends, anymore than they can invent their parents. Life gives these and also takes them away and the great difficulty is to say Yes to life.

Acknowledgments

This book would not have been possible without the help of many good friends and colleagues. First, I would like to thank those persons who read the manuscript itself: Richard Alexander, James T. Carey, Richard Green, Evelyn Hooker, and Robert S. Wallerstein. I have benefited much from their advice, but in no way wish to implicate them—or anyone else, for that matter—in my opinions and conclusions, for which I must take sole responsibility. A number of other colleagues also advised me in regard to the research study of the male homosexual community in the San Francisco Bay Area upon which this book is based and helped me in various ways at different stages of the project: Ernest Becker, Howard S. Becker, Sherri Cavan, Fred Davis, the late Bernice Engle, Erving Goffman, Harold Sampson, Anselm Strauss, and Edward M. Weinshel. Besides thanking her for reading the manuscript, I must also express my gratitude to Evelyn Hooker for encouraging me to enter into work in this area at a time when it was even somewhat more "taboo" than it is now. I would like to thank Lynne Alexander for typing the book through all its drafts, and to gratefully acknowledge the research support of the National Institute of Mental Health of the United States Public Health Service. Through a grant (MH 10903) to the Mount Zion Hospital and Medical Center in San Francisco, both the book and the investigation on which it is based were made possible. To Mount Zion go my thanks for administering the grant with the least possible red tape; in this regard I want especially to acknowledge the assistance of Phyllis Hecker and Helen Boscola.

Finally, but certainly not least, I would like to thank those men who consented to be interviewed for this research study. I have taken care to alter certain biographical items in the case material presented in these pages, so that no one can be identified.

MARTIN HOFFMAN

Berkeley, California
July 1968

Contents

THE GAY WORLD

INTRODUCTION
○
● ●

Homosexuality as a Problem for Science and Society

This book arises out of two experiences on the part of the author. For the past several years (1965–68) I have been engaged in a scientific study of the male homosexual community in the San Francisco Bay Area, under a grant from the National Institute of Mental Health. The more I have studied male homosexuality the more I have become impressed with its seriousness as a social problem; it is perhaps *the most serious undiscussed problem* in the United States today.

Granted that the public discussion of, e.g., the Negro problem has not produced sufficient results toward its solution, nevertheless it is true that we are *aware* of the Negro question as a serious social issue. This, after all, is the first step. The problem of homosexuality, on the other hand, is something which is discussed mostly in the form of gossip and has only within the last several years become an object of legitimate, scientific inquiry. It seemed to me, since the public paid for the conduct of my research, that it was my duty to make clear the social nature of the problem and, therefore, to present my findings to as wide an audience of interested laymen as possible.

The second factor which prompted the writing of this book was the courses about sexual deviance which I taught at the undergraduate and graduate levels at the University of California at Berkeley. In designing courses in this area, it became apparent that there was no satisfactory literature on the problem of male homosexuality which approached it from a broad spectrum of disciplines. There *is* some good literature, but it is almost exclusively written from the point of view of one particular discipline; for example, there are some good psychoanalytic writings on the subject of male homosexuality, but their authors seem to be unaware of the social dimension of the problem and approach it exclusively as a problem of the individual psyche. On the other hand, the late Alfred Kinsey, who contributed notably to the subject, did not take into account the psychodynamic factors in the origin of homosexual behavior, nor did he sufficiently integrate sociological theory into the framework he used to analyze his data. As a result of the fragmentation of knowledge in this area, there does not exist at the present time an adequate general discussion which one can use for teaching purposes.

As a result of these considerations, I decided that rather than presenting my findings only in the form of conventional research reports in learned journals, it would be useful to write a general survey of the problem of male homosexuality in American society from a multi-disciplinary point of view. Invariably when one attempts this kind of approach, the result tends to be somewhat uneven. Although I am a social psychiatrist, and consider myself competent in psychoanalytic theory as well as in the sociology of deviance, there are certainly large areas of knowledge which bear on the problem of male homosexuality in which I have no firsthand experience; consequently, when necessary, I will have to rely on the work done by others. Homosexuality is a problem the understanding of which requires a consideration of knowledge in all the disciplines concerned with human experience, including biology, psychology, sociology, law, psychiatry, history, and also emerging fields which span the conventional disciplines and are not yet very well named.

Among the general perspectives that I want to emphasize in this book, one of them is certainly that the issue of homosexuality cannot adequately be viewed in anything less than an interdisciplinary perspective, and that attempts to see it from the point of view of one specialty alone have led to a grossly unsatisfactory state of knowledge in the field, which has resulted in the failure of modern social science to make a significant contribution to the solution of this serious social issue. Our knowledge about homosexuality is scattered throughout the disciplines and has not been brought together in an integrated way, so that reasonable and useful policy statements could be drawn from this knowledge and could be communicated to the general public in order that, through the American political process, we might begin to deal with what I cannot help regarding as a very unfortunate state of affairs.

The purpose of social psychiatry, if it is to be a meaningful enterprise, must be the identification of those forces in the general society which lead to human unhappiness and mental illness. We social psychiatrists and social scientists must examine how social arrangements create misery in the lives of persons and we must suggest ways of altering the society so that such misery can be decreased. This means that we must begin doing things we have shown little enthusiasm for doing. We must carry the level of our analysis of mental disturbances to a fully social level, to a consideration not only of the internal psychological factors that lead to mental illnesses, but also to an integration of this knowledge with what we know about social processes and about how the society as a whole affects various individuals in such a way as to make them mentally ill. We have been loath to do this (with a few notable exceptions), I think, because to do so means that we must often make clear our opposition to established social conventions. However, a satisfactory analysis of a social problem will almost invariably have implications for existing social arrangements which will suggest some kind of social change to alleviate certain conditions.

Although reluctance to offend the *status quo* is certainly a reason that the psychiatrist does not often take the role of social critic, I believe there is a deeper reason. We are loath to move toward a social psychiatry which is fully social-critical because we are well aware, if only unconsciously, that the American political process is exceptionally slow to respond— when it does respond—to pressing social issues. As psychiatrists, we would generally rather stay in our offices and deal with individual patients, because we feel that here we *can* accomplish something tangible. To venture forth as social critics seems like a genuinely quixotic enterprise, in which the response of the larger society to our analysis of the problems that beset it is most likely to be silence, if not scorn.

And yet we must do it. We must because the thrust of our clinical work requires us to take a broader look at the larger social forces which lead to the clinical problems we see—and to many more that we do not see. Social psychiatry is the logical outgrowth of clinical psychiatric work, and to refuse to create a meaningful social psychiatry because of the perhaps inevitable unresponsiveness of the *status quo* to demands that it alter itself is, simply, to refuse to do our scientific duty.

Freud asked the question this way: "And with regard to any therapeutic application of our knowledge, what would be the use of the most acute analysis of social neuroses, since no one possesses power to compel the community to adopt the therapy?" (1930, p. 142). Of course, he gave his answer *in his work*. He ventured upon such analyses in spite of his doubts about their social effects. In this regard, we must, as we have done in so many other ways, follow Freud's example.

As Laswell has pointed out, social psychiatry is a policy science, "along with law, education and the social disciplines at large" (1962, p. 120). Our very analyses of social problems carry *intrinsically* a mandate for social change. It is in this spirit that the present book was written.

Homosexuality

Just how important is the issue of homosexuality? For a subject which receives so little intelligent public discussion, there is a surprisingly high frequency of homosexual acts. The Kinsey report on male sexual behavior, published in 1948, tells that 37 percent of the total white male population of the United States has at least some overt homosexual experience to the point of orgasm between adolescence and

old age; 25 percent of the male population has *more than
incidental* homosexual experience or reactions for at least
three years between the ages of 16 and 55; 18 percent of
American males have at least as much homosexual as heterosexual experience during their lifetime for a period of at least
three years; 10 percent of all men are *more or less exclusively
homosexual* for at least three years between the ages of 16 and
55. Finally, Kinsey points out that 4 percent of the white males
are exclusively or nearly exclusively homosexual throughout
their entire lives (Kinsey *et al.*, 1948, pp. 650–51).

In spite of some heated controversy surrounding Kinsey's ·
methodology, his studies unquestionably represent the closest
approximation we now have to a comprehensive assessment
of the amounts of the different types of sexual behavior which
exist in the United States today. They indicate that a
tremendous amount of overt homosexual activity occurs between males and that there are many males for whom
homosexuality is not just isolated experiences. Perhaps the
most interesting statistic for our purposes is his finding that
10 percent of American males are more or less exclusively
homosexual for at least three years between the ages of 16 and
55. I suspect that there are few people, including workers in
the social sciences, who are aware that homosexuality among
males exists to such an extent. Since homosexual acts between
consenting adults are illegal in every state in the Union except
Illinois, we seem to have created an enormous number of
criminals, even granting, however, that the laws against
homosexual behavior are only enforced sporadically and very
unevenly and that the police rarely invade private bedrooms,
where most homosexual activity takes place. Nevertheless,
the social sanctions of an extra-legal and quasi-legal nature are ·
so severe that we are here dealing with a problem within the
fabric of American society which involves literally millions of
our citizens.

Since this report will deal primarily with *male* homosexuality, I will very often use the term "homosexuality" as a synonym for this phenomenon and will specifically indicate female homosexuality by using the adjective whenever the subject is referred to. It will be necessary to make some comments about female homosexuality, since we can learn some important things about male behavior from studying the behavior of the female homosexual. I am also going to use a certain amount of homosexual argot in the discussion, since it seems to me that it will portray a more accurate picture of the homosexual scene. Furthermore, I am going to use the slang term "gay" as a synonym for homosexual, though I by no means wish to imply by this use that homosexual life is gay in the more traditional sense of the word.

The research upon which this book is based was specifically designed to study those homosexuals who do not usually become the objects of scientific attention via the psychiatric consulting room or the courts of law. It was a study of the homosexual as he exists in his "natural milieu," i.e., in the gay world and in the larger "straight" society of which that world is a part. At the time of writing, I had interviewed 157 homosexual men, spoken informally with many more, and had spent many hours in social settings where homosexuals congregate (particularly in private homes and in gay bars).

By starting with several homosexuals who were personal acquaintances willing to assist in the research, I was able to meet the men I studied. I particularly looked for men who were reasonably conventional in all but their sexual activities; I soon found that there were more of such individuals than I could ever talk with, even were I to spend the rest of my life doing this study. Homosexual men come from every walk of life, every socioeconomic and religious group, every occupational category. By following out linkages in friendship networks, I was able to meet a wide range of individuals, with varying life-styles, very few of whom would be readily identifiable as gay by the average citizen.

Methodology

At this point we must discuss a serious methodological issue in the present investigation. The research has been done as an ethnographic field study, using the kind of data-gathering technique which a social anthropologist might use if he went into a foreign country in order to study a town or a tribe which was of interest to him. However, the homosexual community is a kind of community which is not defined so much by geographical factors (although homosexuals tend very often to live in certain sections of the city rather than in others) as by certain common values and behaviors, and by shared public places. It is not possible to have any definite idea of the size of the homosexual community by using the methods of such a field study. The reader should bear in mind that all my data on incidence of homosexual behavior have been derived from the Kinsey volume, which was a large-scale, quantitative study of sexual behavior among American males in general. It is only possible to discover the extent and dimensions of homosexual feelings and practices in the population at large by using the kind of method which Kinsey did; namely, to study a cross section of the entire population. It is *not* possible to uncover such data by an ethnographic field study. The purposes of the latter approach are quite different; that is, what I wanted to do was to find out what the homosexual world looked like, and describe its texture and color. It was not my intention to *measure* it in any way. When talking with individuals and groups about the results of my research, I have typically been asked questions which should really only be asked of a scientist who is doing a large-scale survey of the entire population, for it is only such an individual who could answer the quantitative questions which have been asked of me.

For example, people usually want to know what percentage of homosexuals go to gay bars, either regularly or occasionally. It is impossible to answer that question with precision unless one has access to a large random sample of the homosexual population. Clearly, one cannot obtain access to a random sample of this population by doing an ethnographic field study, and thus, this kind of question cannot be answered except by guesswork.

Let us, however, try to make a guess as to the answer. We could say that on a Saturday night, between the hours of midnight and 1:00 A.M., when the number of patrons in most gay bars reaches its peak, there might be something like 6,000 male homosexuals in the approximately 40 gay bars in San Francisco. This figure is based on the speculation, made by an informant very knowledgeable about the San Francisco bar scene, that if an average is taken, there might be 150 homosexuals in each of the 40 bars, although obviously we know this is only the roughest of estimates. But it does give us some idea of the order of magnitude, i.e., it is probably to be measured in terms of *four figures*. Now we know that the homosexual population of the San Francisco Bay Area, which is a geographical area containing approximately 3,000,000 inhabitants (plus numerous bar-going tourists), is a good deal larger than that which could be measured in four figures. Since we know that approximately 4 percent of the American white male population is exclusively homosexual throughout their lives and that 10 percent of the male population is more or less exclusively homosexual for at least three years between the ages of 16 and 55, we can see that the order of magnitude of the population that might be expected to possibly find its way into a gay bar is probably somewhere between 50,000 and 100,000 for the Bay Area. Thus, it becomes immediately clear that the number of people in the gay bars is just a small fraction of the total male homosexual population in the Bay Area. However, we have no idea at all as to how many people go to the bars only occasionally; I have interviewed many people who do go only from time to time. Therefore, there is simply no way of knowing what proportion of that larger population will sometime during the year find its way into one of the bars. We also have no data on bar turnover during a particular evening; but we know enough about the bars to unhesitatingly state that considerably more men enter San Francisco gay bars during an evening than are to be found there during the midnight to 1:00 A.M. peak. For example, there are some gay bars which serve dinner; they have their maximum crowd at 7:00–10:00 P.M. Some of this turnover is counterbalanced by bar-hopping, but this latter factor may not entirely offset the former variable.

I have engaged in this quantitative digression simply to show how very difficult it is to make anything but the roughest estimate of quantitative factors involved in the study of homosexual behavior, unless one is engaged in a large-scale survey. As a matter of fact, one of the most damaging criticisms that can be made against much of the literature in this area of study is that numbers are used where they should not be. That is, writers who have access to a small, non-random sample of homosexuals will quote numbers and percentage figures in a manner which gives the reader the impression that these figures have some relation to the larger population. Yet almost always this is *not* the case, for most of the authors derive their information from voluntary informants, such as those who find their way into a psychiatrist's office, or who are willing to be interviewed by a social scientist. Therefore, to engage in the use of percentages and proportions is usually extremely misleading, since it gives the spurious impression that the conclusions which the writer draws from these percentages and proportions can be generalized to cover a much wider population. I have elsewhere criticized a book by the English social psychologist Michael Schofield for doing just this (Hoffman, 1966).

I have gone at length into this matter because I want to make it very clear to the reader that no claim is made here for conclusions about the homosexual world which are based on a *complete* view of it, i.e., a view which sees all aspects of it fully and in their proper proportion. The fact is that no such view exists and that any writer who claims such a view is engaging in a deception.

But, I would assert, the implications which flow from the admitted limitations of this study are not quite as serious as might first appear. For, after all, what is the *purpose* of such a study? Clearly, the purpose of any piece of social research must be, in the ultimate analysis, to advance the cause of man's well-being by providing information upon which he can act. Therefore, the emphasis must be upon aspects of the subject matter which are socially *problematic*, i.e., which are implicated in the creation of human unhappiness. For a social psychiatrist, it is natural to explore those aspects of homosexuality which constitute a social problem, which lead to mental illness, and which are related to defects in the social arrangements that presently exist in society. Social psychiatry is really a branch of preventive medicine. When physicians study tobacco, they don't need to know *everything* about tobacco. The first thing they need to know is whether or not the smoking of this substance will lead to health problems. If they find that it does, as they have indeed found, then they know what recommendations to make to the public. Likewise, when we study the homosexual world we are going to look for the troublesome areas within it, and therefore, even if we cannot have a fully representative view of this world, it suffices for our purposes if we can have that degree of understanding of it which will lead us to make recommendations as to what can be done to solve these problems. In other words, even though we can't know everything about homosexuality, if we are able to gain enough knowledge to enable us to discern what needs to be done to decrease the human suffering connected with the homosexual world—of which there is plenty—we can know that something worthwhile has been accomplished. Let us, then, proceed to our study of the gay world—its character, its internal structure, and the problems which are generic to it.

1

○
● ●

A Friday Night
and Its Past

On a Friday evening in 1966, at about 11:15 P.M., Tom
entered one of San Francisco's approximately 40 gay bars.
He had never been there before but had heard about it from
some of his friends with whom he played poker regularly on
Wednesday nights. One of them had gone into the bar by
mistake a couple of weeks before and the subject was mentioned as a sort of joke around the poker table; no one suspected that Tom might have been interested in finding out
about the bar. No one would have had any idea at all that
Tom had any homosexual interests. He was 27, fairly good-
looking, married, and the father of four children. He worked

as a truck driver for a bakery in one of the suburbs of San Francisco.

The bar was quite crowded by the time Tom got there, and among those present was David, a 21-year-old blond who was a regular patron of this particular bar. He had come there with friends, after having been to dinner in one of their apartments. David was quite attractive, one might almost say "pretty," and it is possible that a number of people might have suspected that he was homosexual. There was, however, nothing flagrant or "faggoty" about him, although he was rather soft-spoken, mild, and had no particular interest in women. He worked as a clerk in a brokerage office, and had a number of friends, a few of whom might be identifiable as obvious homosexuals. But this was by no means true of the majority of his associates. He was in many respects (and in this unlike Tom) a typical young urban homosexual male. He had come to the bar mainly for the purpose of being with his friends, although he had the thought in the back of his mind that perhaps he might meet somebody with whom he could spend the night. Tom came with the explicit purpose of picking up someone.

Tom, unlike David, felt very uneasy in the bar, since he had never been in a gay bar before. He had had a number of previous homosexual experiences, but this was his first encounter with the gay world *per se*. The first thing he did was order a double martini, which calmed his nerves. Walking into a gay bar is a momentous act in the life history of a homosexual, because in many cases it is the first time he publicly identifies himself as a homosexual. Of equal importance is the fact that it brings home to him the realization that there are many other young men like himself and, thus, that he is a member of a community and not the isolate he had previously felt himself to be. Since San Francisco is a fairly sophisticated city where gay bars are often the subject of comment in the newspapers, since by 1966 several of the public media had begun to discuss homosexuality in a way that was considerably more open and sympathetic than the coverage which it had received ten years before, and since Tom had had some previous homosexual experience, he was not exactly surprised by what he saw; but nevertheless it made a distinct impression on him. Standing in a room with over a hundred men who shared the same sexual orientation he did, he felt the stigma of public identification for the first time in his life.

By the time Tom had finished his martini, he had developed enough courage to walk over to David, to whom he was attracted, and make a conversational opener. Tom began the conversation by asking David about the bar, and David's quite friendly response led him to believe that he might have some chance of getting him to come home to bed with him. Soon David detached himself from his group of friends and began talking with Tom alone. They exchanged some biographical information, although not their last names. Last names are characteristically not mentioned in gay bar conversations because of the wish to preserve a certain degree of anonymity in what is clearly an illicit situation. They told each other what their occupations were, although they did not give the names of the firms for which they worked. Tom told David that he was married and this increased David's attraction to Tom, since he equated heterosexual potency (something he did not possess) with "masculinity," which he, and most homosexuals, consider the single most desirable feature of their partners. While David was not one of those homosexuals who is especially after "straight" males, the prospect of going to bed with a heterosexual or, at any rate, a bisexual male distinctly appealed to him. At about 12:30 A.M. David asked Tom if he would like to come over to his place for a drink (the classic homosexual proposal), and at this point they left the bar and went to David's apartment. They would have had to go to David's place in any case, since Tom could not have taken David home with *him*. David lived with a roommate in the Nob Hill section of San Francisco. There was no sexual relationship between the two, although at one time they had had a brief sexual affair, during the course of which they became friends. David's roommate was out for the evening, and so Tom and David sat in the living room and listened to some records while they had another drink. They exchanged some more biographical information and then David asked Tom about his homosexual interests, for although Tom was the older, David was much more experienced in the practices of the gay world and was able to take the lead in this conversation. Tom asked David a lot of questions about gay life and found out about other bars and about the baths, the parks, and the gay sections of the beach.

After they had talked for about half an hour, David initiated necking and the two young men began kissing and exploring each other's bodies, although they kept their clothes on for about another 15 minutes. David was quite sexually experienced, but Tom had never kissed another man, since his previous homosexual encounters were limited to direct genital contact. This was a much more "romantic" setting than he had previously been used to. He was, however, quite sexually excited by this new activity and soon suggested that they go to bed, which they did.

When they got to bed, they continued necking and petting, until finally Tom made it clear that he wanted to perform fellatio on David. He indicated his wish by gestures rather than by conversation, i.e., he first fondled David's penis, and then began to move his head in the direction of David's pelvic area, and finally began to fellate him. This is something Tom had done before, something he especially liked to do. It was, as a matter of fact, with this act in mind that Tom went to the gay bar in the first place. David ejaculated in about 15 or 20 minutes, after which they both lay in bed for a while, and engaged in some light necking. After a few more minutes, David asked Tom if he would screw him, which, although Tom did not especially want to do, he consented to. When this was over, they both lit up cigarettes and lay in bed smoking for a while.

David asked Tom if he wanted to spend the night with him, but Tom said no, he had to go back and sleep with his wife. He told David that he had told his wife he was going out for a few drinks with the boys, and as it was getting to be about 3:00 in the morning, he had better get going. David gave Tom his phone number and Tom said he would call him, although he never did.

I got the story of this evening's happenings from David, who said he was not sure why Tom never called him back, but that this is not at all unusual in the gay world. He never saw Tom again. It happened, by strange coincidence, that I actually met Tom some months after I had interviewed David, and so I was able to get the story of not only that Friday evening's incident, but also of the past histories of the two men. Neither David nor Tom knew that I had interviewed the other, although I don't really think it would have made much difference to them.

Tom

Tom is a native Californian. Born in Sacramento, he moved to the San Francisco Bay Area when he was eight. He is an only child and lived with his parents until the time he got married at the age of 19. His father is a carpenter and his mother a housewife. He was closer to his mother than to his father, although he now feels that his mother was excessively dominant and in fact describes her as a non-poisonous jellyfish, in that she envelops you, and only later do you realize that this relationship has altered your perceptions. There was a lot of sex play going on when he was a child and he engaged in both homosexual and heterosexual play up to the beginning of adolescence. At this time, heterosexual sex play came under severe social prohibition and he continued with only homosexual play. He has, however, always considered himself more interested in girls and thinks that his interest in men is mostly centered on performing fellatio on them. This is a phenomenon which perplexes him, since he does not understand why he has this feeling. He speculates that it may be related to the emphasis on masculinity in his family, especially on the part of his father, which he was never quite able to live up to. His father had been a fairly successful high school athlete and encouraged Tom to go out for sports and compete with the other boys, which he did, but not nearly so successfully as his father. Tom says he thinks that, somehow, because of this, he became caught up with the idea of masculinity and became interested in the male genital. When we come to discuss the genesis of homosexuality in a later chapter, we will see how well this phenomenon is explained by psychoanalytic theory.

In spite of this desire to perform fellatio, Tom states that his predominant sexual interest was always oriented toward girls, and he began having sexual relations with a girl friend at 17. He married at 19 and is now the father of two boys and two girls. He describes his marriage as a fairly satisfactory one, although he says he is not romantically in love with his wife. Nevertheless, he does feel that he gets along with her pretty well. She has no suspicions that he has any homosexual interests and is very naïve about the subject. Interestingly enough, he has never had sex relations with a woman outside of marriage and, to his knowledge, his wife has been faithful. He feels that to commit heterosexual adultery would be "cheating" on his wife in a way that his homosexual adventures are not, and he is somehow able to bracket off this homosexual interest into a completely different compartment of his life and thought.

Tom had some homosexual experiences throughout high school, but really became aware of homosexuality as an entity and identified himself as having homosexual interests only when he went into the service in his early 20's. At first, he tried to repress this interest, but finally he succumbed and began to perform fellatio occasionally. His contacts have mostly been in public rest rooms and, less often, on the beach. Not until the night he met David did he become aware of the gay world as an organized entity which he could relate to his own interests. Since that time, when he did go home with and spend some time in bed with another man, he has gone back to gay bars on a number of occasions and has picked up a number of different men. In no case has he had sex with the same man more than once, for he somehow feels a loss of interest in the partner after he has performed fellatio on him.

Tom is not sure exactly how he should view his own homosexual feelings. He doesn't quite define himself as a homosexual, for he feels that in order to be a "true homosexual," one has to have no interest in women. He seems not to have too much guilt about his activities. He is afraid, to a slight degree, that he might get into trouble sometime if he has sex in a public place and is arrested, but now that he has discovered the world of the gay bars and the baths, he has given up his interest in meeting people in men's rooms and out in the open, so that he feels he has decreased the probability of any trouble with the law. Once every few months he gets a strong urge to have sex with another man and then he will go down to a bar or a bath and meet a partner. At his present age, he is attractive and young enough to find suitable partners, but he thinks that maybe when he gets older he will have to pay for the privilege of performing fellatio on a young man. He is aware of the hustling scene, but has not yet become a customer of the male prostitutes in the city.

Tom thinks of his homosexual interest as rather peculiar, but he does not define himself as troubled or mentally ill. He feels that, except for the slight legal risk, there is nothing wrong with his interest and he does not feel that there is any danger of his wife or friends finding out about it. The rest of his life might be described as extremely conventional and he has none of the interests that homosexuals not infrequently have (but which they do not, of course, uniformly have), such as an interest in the arts or the theater or clothes or interior decoration. He is a typical lower-middle-class family man with rather ordinary interests in certain sports like bowling and football. He plays poker, watches television, goes out with his wife to the movies or to visit his family, plays with the children, and generally feels fairly content with his life. His homosexuality he regards as rather peripheral to his general life and does not feel that it impinges in any way on his normal round of daily activities.

It would never occur to Tom that he should seek psychiatric treatment for homosexuality. He is the kind of homosexual who would never appear in a psychiatrist's office and, typically, would never run into any trouble with the law. His friends, neighbors, and employers would never think of him as homosexual. The fact that he is neither effeminate nor

indiscreet in his selection of places for meeting sexual partners, and also the fact that he is heterosexually married and
leads an otherwise conventional life, completely hides his
homosexuality from all those who know him either socially
or vocationally.

Tom's homosexual partners never know his full identity
nor does he attempt to have any further contact with them
after the sexual act is over. Although he is sometimes to be
found in the gay world, he is not wholly part of it, since he
does not have any interest in the social aspects of gay life.
For him it is simply a meeting place for potential sexual
partners. He does not become involved in the round of
parties, bar-hopping, and friendship networks that form part
of the gay community. It was actually only by chance that I
was able to interview him. He happened to be talking with
an acquaintance of mine, in a gay bar, whom he was interested in going to bed with. This acquaintance knew of my
work and told him about it, and he agreed to be interviewed.

There is no question that there are a lot of married men,
like Tom, who engage in homosexual practices from time to
time. They are difficult to get to for purposes of interviewing,
but anyone who is involved at all in homosexual life will tell
you that he has met and had sex with a fair number of them.
One way in which the social scientist runs across them is
if they come to a psychiatrist or other professional person
for help, or if they are arrested. But those who enter into the
view of social science through one of these two channels are
only a minority, and perhaps a very atypical minority, of the
people who fall into the category of heterosexually married
homosexuals.

It is worthwhile emphasizing to the reader that the common stereotype of the homosexual as the effeminate, limp-
wristed, obvious fairy is indeed a stereotype, and applies to

only a small minority of the American male homosexual population. I chose to present Tom's case first, in this book, because I would like to make this stereotype vanish from the reader's mind, since if it is present there, he will not be able to understand what gay life is really about. What is worthwhile emphasizing is that although Tom is sexually attracted to and desirous of sexual contact with other men, and consequently defines himself, to *some* extent, as homosexual, in all other respects he is a typical American family man. That there are millions of non-identifiable male homosexuals—many of them, like Tom, completely unsuspected by anyone around them—should certainly make us pause, for it is clear that our present social attitude is completely unaware of, and thus unable to deal intelligently with, problems which might result from this kind of sexual orientation.

David

David came to San Francisco from Kansas City when he was 20 years old. His father was a dentist and his mother a housewife. He has no brothers, but has a sister three years older than him and one two years younger.

He first noticed an erotic interest in boys when he was around 12 years old, but did not consider having sex with them until he was 18. At this time he became involved in a theatrical group in his home town and he was introduced to a number of homosexuals. From them he learned the terminology of the homosexual community and was introduced to a few novels about the subject. He was befriended by someone whom he describes as a "gay mother," who sort of took it upon himself to instruct David in the ways of the gay world and told him that eventually he would "come out," i.e., define himself as homosexual and enter the homosexual world. This person was not sexually interested in David, but there was someone whom he described to David as being an admirer of his. At a party, this admirer kissed David, who liked it and got an erection. But when the seducer learned that David was still a virgin, he decided not to have sex with him, not wishing to be the first one to introduce him to homosexual practices. For a year David associated with homosexuals in this theatrical group, but did not engage in any overt sexual behavior.

It took him about a year, he says, to finally and definitely think of himself as homosexual. He went to college at the age of 19 and had his first homosexual experience, with his college roommate, whom he had a crush on. His first sexual experience consisted of necking and allowing his roommate to perform fellatio on him. He now says that he will engage in almost any kind of sexual activity, but he has found out that his preference is to play the passive role in anal intercourse. He remarks that, unlike so many of his gay friends, he never had any adolescent homosexual play. He says that he began masturbating at the age of 14, after a friend had told him about it. He says that he immediately had homosexual fantasies, but they were of a rather vague kind and they involved no specific homosexual contact, merely the picture of an attractive male in his mind. He has never been physically attracted to women. He has necked with them, but it never really did anything for him. He says that he simply does not feel sexually attracted to girls, although he does appreciate, in an intellectual way, that a girl can be attractive.

David decided to drop out of college in his home town and come to San Francisco, largely because of difficulties with his parents. One of his gay friends wrote a letter to him which his parents opened, and they became upset. They sent him to a psychiatrist, who concluded that David was not really interested in changing his sexual orientation, and the psychiatrist wound up telling the parents to read the Kinsey report. This apparently stymied them and they didn't know what to do. But David felt that there was so much tension at home that he ought to leave the house. He decided that he would come to San Francisco, because he had heard that it had a reputation as being fairly tolerant toward homosexuals. He had thought of moving to Chicago, which is also a large urban center in which there is a fairly active gay community, but he figured that if he was going to move, he might as well come to a warmer climate.

David came to San Francisco carrying with him the names of some of the gay bars. He began to frequent them and soon formed a circle of acquaintances. Since he is fairly attractive, he found that gay life was interesting and emotionally, as well as sexually, gratifying. He met his roommate in one of the bars and had an affair with him for about a month, but this seemed to dissolve, and they no longer have any sexual interest in each other. He considers himself not too promiscuous, because he does not engage in any sexual activity in any public places, such as rest rooms or parks, and will only have sex with someone he has met and conversed with.

David seems fairly content with his present life, but he does say that he thinks he will have a problem when he gets older and is not so attractive. He would like to find a permanent partner with whom he could settle down, but he knows that this is not a very frequent occurrence in the gay world. He has met a number of couples, but they form the exception rather than the rule so far as he has been able to observe. He says that maybe the thing for him to do is get out of his mind the idea of a "special thing" with some one person. David says that he is quite selective in choosing partners, and he often rejects people in whom he is not interested. As a result, he does not have as much sex as he would like. He has sex about once or twice a week, and while sometimes he will have sex with the same person more than once, in general, his sexual relationships are on a one-night-stand basis. He says he does not feel lonely because he has a circle of friends, but he thinks maybe he would like to have something more substantial a little bit later on in life.

David thinks one of the reasons that he has given up the idea of going to college is his involvement in gay life. He says that he now likes to go out at least several times a week to participate in the round of parties and bar-going which his friends like to do, and he thinks that he would not have the ability to stay home and study, which would be required if he went back to school. David seems to have some regret about not going back to college, since he has met a number of professional people in the homosexual world and he feels intellectually inferior to them, although this is compensated for by the fact that he is considered by them to be quite attractive and is much sought after as a sexual partner.

David says that he is not particularly sorry that he is homosexual, although he doesn't like the fact that he is estranged from his family. He says that if he had had the choice, he would have preferred to have been heterosexual, but that at the present time, he is fairly content with his lot and finds the gay world interesting and eventful. He likes the idea of being courted and sought after and obviously finds a great deal of narcissistic gratification in the gay bar scene. He thinks that if he settled down with a lover at the present time, he might actually find that kind of life rather dull in comparison to the bar scene, since he would be spending most of his time at home, would not be going out so much, and even if he did go out with his lover, would not find himself in the role

of someone being courted. He thinks the laws against homosexual behavior are stupid, but doesn't feel particularly
affected by them, since he does nothing that would bring
him into conflict with the law. He says that he can't understand how his friends who engage in sexual behavior in public
can take the risk.

In many respects, David is a typical habitué of gay bar
society. He is young, attractive, promiscuous, interested in the
superficial glamour of the gay world, and likes very much
being desired by other men. He has never had any interest in
women, and it would seem the chances of his developing
heterosexual interest are very low. He does not even consider
this as a possibility for the future. At the present time, he is
fairly well adjusted to his social setting, but it is obvious that
he is going to face some severe problems in the future and he
is dimly aware of this, although he tries not to think about
it very much. In about five to ten years, his boyish good looks
will have begun to fade, and he will find himself in a considerably less valued role in the gay community. Since he has
not really prepared himself vocationally, he is not going to
have an interesting career to occupy his attention. It is possible that he will be able to form a relationship with someone
which is more intimate than any relationship he has now,
but it seems unlikely that it will be a sexual one. This is, at
least in part, because he has done nothing, and is not
interested at present in doing anything, toward trying to
develop a capacity for intimacy by attempting to participate
in a close relationship with another man which includes sex.
Later on in this book we want to explore some of the reasons
which lie behind this kind of disinclination for closeness in
people like David. However, certainly one of the powerful
factors militating against David's trying such an emotional
venture is the very structure of the gay world itself, which

provides so many sexual and psychological temptations to an attractive young man and thus really encourages promiscuity and transitory interpersonal contacts.

In closing this chapter, I think it is appropriate to point out that both David and Tom, in their own separate ways, while very well adjusted to the gay world in the present stage of their lives, are in fact going to have to make some considerable changes in their style of life, since they won't really be able to continue to live indefinitely as they are now doing. Since Tom has a stable family setting of his own and can probably pay for occasional sexual partners, even as he becomes less attractive, his problem is probably the less severe of the two. David, on the other hand, is clearly going to have to make some real and serious changes in his entire life-style if he is to cope with the advancing years. It is a tribute to human adaptability that people are able to make such changes, but if one thing is clear, it is that society has really made no provision to help such individuals.

2

○
● ●

What Is Homosexuality?

I am going to use the term "homosexual" in this book to refer to those individuals who have a sexual attraction toward partners of the same sex, over at least a few years of their lives. It should, however, be made clear that there is no definition of "homosexual" or "homosexuality" which is going to be agreed to by 100 percent of the scientists working in this field. Kinsey, for example, objects to using the term "homosexual" or "heterosexual" even as an adjective to describe persons, and prefers to reserve these words to describe the nature of the overt sexual relations or of the stimulae to which the individual erotically responds (1948, p. 617). Yet, a few pages later in this same book, he sets up a heterosexual-homosexual rating scale, which includes both psychological reactions and overt experience and in which individuals are rated, for example, as "predominantly homosexual, but more than incidentally heterosexual." So we see that Kinsey himself is forced into using the term as an adjective to describe persons. I think that there is no way that we can talk intelligently about the subject without speaking of individuals as homosexuals. To avoid doing so would be to sacrifice any attempt at a common understanding of the subject to a merely quantified study of overt behavior. Even Kinsey, who was himself most sympathetic to a taxonomic approach to sexuality, does not quite do this. It would certainly behoove those of us who wish to arrive at a broad socio-psychological understanding of the phenomenon to adhere to the common-sense use of the terms, at least insofar as they can be made serviceable.

When I use the term "homosexual" to describe a man, by this I do not mean that he may not also be heterosexual, for I think there are a significant number of people, such as Tom, who are sexually attracted to and seek out sexual partners of both sexes. These people we could very conveniently call bisexual, and I will do so, providing only that it is understood that the nature of the sexual attraction to men may not be the same as the sexual attraction to women. In other words, just because we say that Tom is sexually attracted to both men and women does not imply that his feelings on seeing a man and his feelings on seeing a woman are the same. In both cases he may be sexually stimulated, but his entire perception of the situation may be quite different, and his behavior with men—both in bed and out—may be of an altogether different kind than his behavior with women.

We saw in the last chapter how Tom's sexual interest in men was almost entirely directed toward performing fellatio and that he engaged in foreplay and other sexual acts with his partner simply in order to satisfy the partner. When Tom goes to bed with his wife, on the other hand, he *is* interested in extensive foreplay and *is* interested in having conventional sexual intercourse with her. His feeling toward women is much more of a warm and enveloping kind in which he ultimately (in fantasy) wants to mingle his body with that of his partner. With men, on the other hand, he feels as if sucking his partner's penis will be very exciting and he can somehow derive a peculiar kind of satisfaction from this activity, the nature of which is not entirely clear to him. I think, therefore, that when we use the term "homosexual" to describe Tom, we must be clear that he is also heterosexual, and when we use the term "bisexual" to describe him we must be completely clear, as many writers are not, that we are talking about two very different kinds of feeling and behavioral states.

What I am saying here, in effect, is that there are many different kinds of homosexuals and many different kinds of bisexuals. We might also add that there are many different kinds of heterosexuals. This will hopefully become clearer when we come to the discussion of the genesis of homosexuality. In asking the question "Why is a man homosexual?" we do not wish to imply by any means that this is to be regarded as a basically different kind of question from "Why is a man heterosexual?" Virtually all the literature on homosexuality is marred by the failure of its authors to take account of the fact that heterosexuality is just as much a problematic situation for the student of human behavior as is homosexuality. The only reason it does not seem to us a problem is because we take its existence for granted. However, we should know enough about science by now to realize that it is just those questions we take for granted that are the ones, when properly asked, which would open up new areas of scientific exploration. The question should really be put as follows: "Why does a person become sexually excited (i.e., in the case of a man, why does he get an erection) when confronted with a particular kind of stimulus?" If the question is asked in this way it can be seen that heterosexuality is just as much of a problem as homosexuality, in the scientific if not in the social sense.

The fact is that there are almost as many different kinds of homosexual, bisexual, and heterosexual responses as there are individuals. On the other hand, there *are* a number of common features which characterize large groups of individuals, so that we *can* make generalizations about particular kinds of response. Obviously, Tom's wish for fellatio and David's wish to hold another man close to him are not unique, but are shared by a sufficient number of other men so that in fact they have already been described and very convincing explanations of them have already been given in the psychiatric literature. We will come to these explanations in a later chapter.

Incidence

In the Introduction, in order to make the point that homosexuality is a social problem of enormous proportions, I discussed the incidence figures on male homosexual behavior from the 1948 Kinsey report. The figures that I think are particularly significant are the following: "4 percent of the white males are exclusively homosexual throughout their lives, after the onset of adolescence" (1948, p. 651). This figure, which refers to at least 4,000,000 American males, tells us that there is a very significant number of men who are exclusively homosexual, both in regard to their overt experience and their psychic reactions. These are people like David, who never have any interest in having sexual relations with a woman. They constitute a considerable part of those individuals who make up the most visible portion of the gay world. However, because 10 percent of the American male population is more or less exclusively homosexual for *at least* three years between the ages of 16 and 55 (Kinsey, 1948, p. 651), a significant number of those men who are to be seen in the visible sector of the gay world, e.g., in the bars, are not exclusively homosexual for their whole lives. This added 6 percent includes those individuals who, at the very least, have three years during their late adolescent or adult lives in which, although they may have incidental experience with the opposite sex, and sometimes react psychically to members of the opposite sex, are almost entirely homosexual in their overt activities and/or their reactions. This 6 percent includes a substantial number of men who have had some trial heterosexual experience but who have then become exclusively gay. It is probably this figure which deserves the most emphasis, because it indicates how very widespread male homosexuality is. Kinsey pointed out that those who are more or less exclusively gay for at least three years represent approximately one male in ten in the white male population. The journalist Jess Stearn once wrote a book called *The Sixth Man*, which gave the idea that one out of every six American men was gay. This, of course, was pooh-poohed and I remember that when I first saw the book's title I reacted very skeptically. But, as a matter of fact, if one looks at Kinsey's figures, one finds that 18 percent of the males have at least as much homosexual as heterosexual experience in their lives for at least three years between the ages of sixteen and fifty-five. This is more than one in six of the white male population (Kinsey, 1948, p. 650).

Individual Types

What kind of men are these homosexuals? What do they look like? How do they act? To these questions one can only give the most general (and unsatisfactory) answer, namely, that these people run the entire gamut from the swishy faggot who can be identified a block away, to the husband, son, or brother whom even the fairly sophisticated person would not suspect of any homosexual interest. They include people who are handsome, clever, and rich, those who are ugly, stupid, and poor, and all combinations and gradations in between. Homosexuality penetrates into every conceivable socioeconomic, religious, and geographical classification. There *are* some slight differences, however. For example, Kinsey found that the highest rate of homosexual behavior occurs among those males who go to high school but not beyond. It is also quite true that homosexuals migrate to large urban centers, so that there is probably a higher percentage of practicing homosexuals in Los Angeles than in Bakersfield, California. But these minor differences do not obviate the more significant fact that homosexuals are to be found throughout the entire nation in all social strata.

A great deal of nonsense has been written in the scientific literature about "active" and "passive," "masculine" and "feminine" homosexuals. The implication is often made that there is a sharp difference between these two kinds of individuals. It is certainly true that there is a minority of homosexual men who can be classified both from the point of view of their own conscious definition of themselves as masculine or feminine and from the point of view of what they will do or not do in bed. But this is true only for a minority. The fact is that most homosexuals cannot be so classified and, in fact, will generally take a great variety of roles in sexual performance. Evelyn Hooker has arrived at the same conclusion from her detailed study of 30 predominantly or exclusively homosexual males whom she has intensively interviewed over a period of eight years (Hooker, 1965a). She found that the consciousness of masculinity or femininity on the part of her research subjects appeared to bear no clear relation to particular sexual patterns, and that for the majority of individuals in her sample, there was no apparent correspondence between a conscious sense of identity as masculine or feminine and a preferred or predominant role during the sexual act. This does not mean that these men don't have preferred sexual patterns. They do. But these patterns do not, with a very few exceptions, bear any relationship to their conscious sense of themselves as "masculine" or "feminine."

Granted, then, that homosexuals do a lot of different things in bed, just what exactly do they do? Most American investigators have found that there are four "classic" positions in which an individual might find himself engaged when he is in bed with another male. These can be divided into oral and anal and then again into insertor or receptor roles, so that an individual may be an oral insertor, an anal insertor, an oral receptor, or an anal receptor. He can also engage in mutual fellatio (69) and can engage in a great deal of alternation among these roles.

Curiously enough, the English social psychologist, Michael Schofield, found that the largest proportion of homosexuals who were members of the English homosexual community which he studied (using roughly the same kind of ethnographic methods which Hooker and I have used) prefer "genital apposition," or very close body contact without penetration of a body orifice as the means to ejaculation (Schofield, 1965). The term "rub-off" is sometimes used to refer to this method of achieving orgasm. The individual simply rubs his penis against his partner's body, for example, against his belly or his leg. Schofield's finding is in quite sharp contrast to what all investigators would agree is the sexual preference of American male homosexuals, who by and large think of this technique as rather adolescent and generally prefer one or more variations of either oral or anal insertion. Why this curious national contrast exists has never been explained, and, as a matter of fact, it has not really even been noticed. I am not going to attempt an explanation of it here, but I think it is certainly something which is at least very curious and might even be an indicator, especially if it can be verified by other English investigators, of a quite different attitude toward sexuality across the ocean.

In classifying homosexual sex behavior in this way, we cannot, of course, really give the reader a feeling for the immense variation that exists in sexual practices, both among individuals and, to a lesser but significant extent, within the *same* individual over a period of time. It must be emphasized that people *learn* sexual behavior just as they learn any other form of complex activity. Thus, the sexual preferences and sexual repertory of an individual who has been "out" for five years is going to be quite different from that which he had at the time of his first experience. Or perhaps this statement might be qualified: these factors may very well be quite different, but they are not necessarily different. For some people stick to the very same preference that they began with. Some people find out right away what they "really" like, but

with others it takes much more time. Some of them are
never sure. Both Bieber (1962) and Hooker (1965a) have
reported that there is a substantial number of homosexuals
who express no sexual preference. That is, they do not prefer
one sexual act to another. My own interviews have yielded
a different result and I have been somewhat at a loss to
explain this. I have never encountered a male homosexual
who did not express a preference for a particular kind of
sexual act. It seems to me that this discrepancy can be
explained in the following way: Hooker and Bieber, in classifying sexual behavior, have stuck pretty close to the four
"classic" types of sexual activity, i.e., oral and anal insertion,
and they have not included as objects of preference those
kinds of activities which fall outside these four types. In other
words, because the four "classic" types are so standard among
American male homosexuals, some men have been at a loss
to explain what they really like to do in terms of them,
since they really do not like to do one of those four things
best of all. I would guess that when Hooker or Bieber asked
them about this they were somewhat unsure of what to say,
so they said that they didn't know what they liked to do or
said that they really had no preference—that anything would
do. My own interviews indicate that they actually do have a
specific preference but they don't know how to express it.
When they say that they will do anything or that they like
to do anything, what they really mean is that they are quite
willing to go along with their partner's desires, and thus they
will engage in one or more of these four "classic" kinds of
sexual activity. Very often, however, such individuals might
actually prefer simply to go to bed with another man, engage
in necking and petting and close body contact, and might
not really be interested in either achieving orgasm themselves
or in inducing their partner's orgasm. One might say that,

for these individuals, *simply going to bed with another male is the thing they really want.* Obviously, this can be described as sexual, provided it is understood that an ejaculation is not the thing that is most desired. Among these people, one would probably find a number of those whom Schofield has described in his English studies to which we have referred above. Although this does not explain the discrepancy in numbers between the English and American homosexual populations, it does serve, to some extent, to include these individuals in the American figures. In other words, it may be that the American investigators have simply included as "expressing no preference" those whom Schofield would have classified as preferring "genital apposition." (Schofield [1965, p. 112] reports that 42 percent of his sample prefer genital apposition. Hooker [1965a, p. 33] reports that 23 percent of her sample express no preference; and Bieber [1962, p. 233] reports that 24 percent of his sample express no preference.)

Two Roommates

The story of Bob and Danny, who have been living together for about nine months, is a good example of the varied (and sometimes non-preferred) sexual roles homosexuals will utilize in order to achieve different kinds of sexual and non-sexual goals. Bob is 26 years old. He first began engaging in homosexual behavior when he was in college, at the age of 20. He had had substantial heterosexual experience and considered himself a heterosexual, but he was willing to go along with homosexual behavior for reasons which he did not entirely understand. He was willing to do anything in bed in order to please his partner. But he didn't particularly like any form of sexual activity in any special sense. He said that he liked a close relationship with another man, especially an older one, and he was willing to go to bed with him in order to get this kind of relationship. He had a number of affairs with older men, and then he became a male prostitute. By the time he was 22, after he had been hustling for about a year, he realized that he actually liked having fellatio performed on him and he definitely enjoyed the experience of having another man's mouth on his penis. His hustling has continued off and on until the present time. During all this time he has engaged in considerable heterosexual experience and it would appear that in a strictly sexual sense his interest has always been more directed toward women than toward men. However, for psychological reasons, he has had great difficulty in his relationships with women. He is more emotionally comfortable with men, so that he has been continually attracted into homosexual practices, until the point was reached at which he actually began to enjoy them. He really only enjoys the insertor role and prefers being fellated, although if his partner enjoys being screwed, he can work up a certain amount of enthusiasm for this activity as well.

Danny is one of those individuals who always knew what he liked. He began having homosexual experiences at the age of 24. He is now 28. For about ten years prior to his first homosexual experience he had the fantasy, which was especially clear during masturbation, that he wanted to be screwed by another man and he has always adhered to this desire. He found that the practice of this activity was at least as satisfying as the fantasy and he has made no secret of his preference to all his sexual partners. When he and Bob have sex together, which is about once every two weeks, there is no question about what they are going to do in bed. They do not engage in very many preliminaries.

It should be added that by no means do these two men

limit their sexual relationships to each other. Bob is still having heterosexual relations and Danny has numerous other homosexual partners. Danny is quite willing to do other things in bed besides taking the receptor role in anal intercourse, but it is clear what his real preference is. As a matter of fact, he feels that he has become more interested in this kind of activity and less interested in any other type in the four years since he has been out. It should probably be added here that Bob has had a great deal of difficulty in coming to terms with the self-concept of himself as homosexual, a problem which we will want to discuss at some length later on in the book. Danny has not really shown much conscious guilt about his homosexual interests, nor has he let considerations of prudence interfere with his very vigorous search for sexual partners. He has been known to engage in his favorite form of sexual activity in public places, especially parks. It remains to be asked, however, why Danny waited a full ten years after he knew he was gay and knew what he wanted sexually before he engaged in his first homosexual experience. And while this is a question that cannot definitely be answered, it is our opinion that he has in fact been struggling with some of the same kinds of problems on an unconscious level that Bob has been struggling with consciously. Just why he was finally able to throw off what he described as "hesitancy" in approaching other men and develop instead what psychiatrists might call a counter-phobic attitude toward homosexuality, i.e., an overreaction to his previous shyness, is not at all clear. This is, however, a not uncommon thing to find in the biographies of male homosexuals, for quite a considerable number of them have waited a very long time before they engaged in their first sexual act.

Also, for a remarkable number of individuals, including many people who have gone into professions concerned with the study of human behavior, and who are both bright and sensitive, a number of years have elapsed between puberty and the time when they began to become *aware* of their homosexual interests. Although Danny was aware of his homosexual feelings practically since puberty, other individuals who have shown the same overt pattern of behavior, that is, who have not engaged in their first homosexual act until they were well into their 20's, have gone those ten years without ever realizing that they had any interest in other men. A lot of them simply did not feel that they had any interest in girls, but they were never able to feel an active sexual interest in their male schoolmates, nor were they able to define themselves in any way as sexually deviant. We shall want to discuss this curious phenomenon from a theoretical point of view in later chapters.

3

The Public Places
of Gay Life

In this chapter, I want to portray, insofar as a writer of non-fiction can, the kind of social world in which most emerging homosexuals find themselves. The fictional literature in this area is almost uniformly bad and seems to be written purely for newsstand profit. Nevertheless, a really good book, like John Rechy's *City of Night*, shows us that the novelist can convey a feeling for a way of life, foreign to most of us, in a manner which the social scientist cannot hope to duplicate. Rechy's book, the story of a hustler, a male prostitute whose clients are homosexuals, is interesting on several accounts. It presents a beautiful description of the life and psychological problems of such an individual, and at the same time, for those of us who know what gay life is like, it makes us wonder why the life of the hustler is, in some very important respects, so very much like that of the average, middle-class homosexual.

When a young man begins to define himself as homosexual, he is faced with the problem of where to find sexual partners. He will soon discover that there are various public places in which homosexual partners can be found. They are, principally, gay bars, particular steam baths, rest rooms, and certain areas of streets and parks which are known to the homosexual community. To a very large extent, the active homosexual's life revolves around these public places, since he typically finds himself in a constant search for new partners.

As we shall see, one of the most striking features of the homosexual world is the great degree of sexual promiscuity to be found in it. Since the sexual relationships in gay life tend to be transitory, the sexually active homosexual constantly needs new partners in order to obtain a reasonable amount of sexual satisfaction. In response to the need for homosexual meeting places, public places for sexual encounters tend to develop. I don't wish to deny that there do exist some fairly stable homosexual relationships, sometimes called "gay marriages," which last over a period of years; nevertheless, my own experience agrees with Kinsey's findings that: "Long term relationships between two males are notably few" (Kinsey, 1948, p. 633). This question of the stability of paired relationships is one which is debated constantly among homosexuals and is especially a point of disagreement between the homosexual organizations which have sprung up within the last ten years and those authorities in the scientific community who maintain that homosexuality and promiscuity go hand in hand. It should be pointed out that Kinsey was not at all unsympathetic to homosexuals and that he had the benefit of studying a large sample of the general population, so that his statement is the best scientific evidence we now have on this disputed issue.

At this point, I think we should introduce a distinction which is not often made in the literature, namely, between sexual promiscuity (or at any rate, a propensity for sexual promiscuity among males) and an inability to develop close and lasting sexual-interpersonal relationships. Kinsey's statement does not mean that homosexuals are promiscuous, although this is true. What it really means is that they do not form lasting, paired, sexual relationships with each other in the way in which heterosexual couples characteristically do. The reasons for this we will postpone discussing until somewhat later in the book. Nevertheless, it should be made quite clear that sexual promiscuity is one of the most striking, distinguishing features of gay life in America.

Streets, Parks, and Rest Rooms

A competent social ethnographer could write a very detailed description of the activity which goes on in streets, parks, and rest rooms, on the part of male homosexuals. It is not really my intention to do so here, since it is not necessary to write a complete ethnography in order to outline the points which I wish to make. John Rechy's second novel, *Numbers*, contains much detailed ethnographic description of homosexual contacts made in rest rooms and especially in parks. As the reader might well imagine, contacts which are made in such places are characterized by their brevity and their casualness more than by anything else. Homosexuals who meet sexual partners in the street do not have sex with them on the street, but usually adjourn to one of their apartments. In the parks and in the rest rooms, sex right then and there may or may not occur, depending upon the propensities of the two individuals involved. Sometimes a sexual act takes place in the park or in the rest room, and sometimes partners will adjourn to an apartment, although this is more likely the case for park contacts than for rest-room contacts. All these places are under a good deal of surveillance by the police, and the individuals who engage in sexual solicitation and sexual activity there take great risks. For some, this factor of risk unquestionably adds to the excitement of the sexual encounter. Needless to say, the chances of meeting someone with whom one can have a prolonged, satisfactory, personal relationship are not very great, although occasionally such relationships do develop from such brief and casual meetings.

A prominent attorney told how he met the man with whom he has been living for six years by cruising a street in the bohemian section of town. He surveyed all the people walking along the thoroughfare and loitered around some of the store windows, as if he were window-shopping, in order that a possible partner might get the idea that he was interested in making a sexual contact. When he finally attracted the attention of a suitable prospect, the two of them engaged in what one might perhaps regard as a little ceremonial dance, in which they exchanged searching glances and then moved on a little bit to the next store window. Finally, the attorney became somewhat tired of this and walked in the direction of his apartment, which was nearby. He was not sure whether the other man was going to follow him—but he did. The attorney went into his apartment and the other man followed him inside and proceeded immediately to take off his clothes. A sexual encounter followed. No words were spoken until after the sexual experience was over. They were surprised to find that they both had some extra-sexual interests in common and a friendship gradually developed between them. As is so typically the case, the beginning of the relationship was characterized by a sexual affair, but the sexual activity has been terminated, and they now seek sexual partners outside the home.

One of the most curious aspects of the homosexual community—insofar as it may be called a community—is that news travels very fast, and information as to the location of those particular streets, those sections of the public parks, and those particular rest rooms where homosexual contacts may be found becomes rapidly circulated among the active members of the community. When police activity interferes with the sexual meetings in these locales, the places of activity will often switch to another location. Police interference, however, does not always stop homosexuals from cruising in a particular spot. Sometimes it is obvious even to these homosexual men themselves that they find the danger of arrest an inducement to seek sexual excitation in such places.

It is not true that the majority of homosexuals are recognizable on sight by the uninitiated. It is often true, however, that they can recognize each other. This is not because of any distinguishing physical characteristics, but, rather, because when cruising, they engage in behavioral gestures which immediately identify themselves to each other. A large part of cruising is done with the eyes, by means of searching looks of a prolonged nature and through the surveying of the other man's entire body. It is also done by lingering in the presence of the other person, and by glancing backward. After a few minutes of cruising, the prospective partner will readily get the message that someone is interested in him. In rest rooms, protocol for making contacts is based on giving signals to the individual in the next booth, usually done by a tapping of the foot or sometimes by passing notes underneath the partition, or by standing at the urinal for rather long periods of time, fondling one's own penis, then looking at and finally touching the penis of the man at the adjacent spot. Vice-squad officers are, of course, aware of these techniques and make considerable use of them in procuring arrests.

Sometimes homosexuals—when, for example, cruising a park—will make a more direct approach by engaging in direct physical contact with the prospective partner, often by touching his genitals. This approach has at least three serious disadvantages, one being that the other person might not be homosexual and thus be very offended and perhaps stunned by this direct approach, and may resort to physical violence. The second danger is that a police officer could be nearby and view the scene, and an arrest might ensue. Third, even if the other person is a homosexual who is cruising the park, he might not care for such an overt approach and might leave the scene, even though he may have found the person who groped him physically attractive.

The homosexual's expectation in these three public places is for direct sexual contact with a minimum of conversation or social preliminaries, and the implied contract is for immediate sex, either in the public place itself or, directly following, in a private locale. Whether one wants to describe an encounter such as this as a "one-night stand" is a matter of definition. It is certainly no more than that.

The Baths

In certain of the larger cities in America there are steam baths which cater exclusively to male homosexuals. Whether or not these baths are viable commercial institutions depends upon police attitudes, since there is no question that a market for them exists among the male homosexual population. The attitude of police toward such institutions varies widely, from toleration to suppression, just as police attitudes toward gay bars differ from city to city. Some police feel they want no homosexual gathering places in their domain, while other law enforcement agencies feel that homosexuals should be allowed to segregate in their own public, but enclosed, places in order to prevent them from becoming a nuisance in the more open areas which we have described above. It is said that proprietors of establishments such as baths and gay bars pay off police for the privilege of running their businesses; I have no direct evidence on this question. In any case, it would seem that even if such payoffs do occur, they only occur within the framework of an already established police policy of toleration. To my knowledge, there exists nothing even approaching a satisfactory study of how attitudes are developed on the part of police agencies toward homosexuals and the relation between these attitudes and actual police practice. One thing is clear, and that is that cities vary widely in the reception which they afford to homosexual activity. Consequently, homosexuals frequently move from more repressive cities and towns into areas where there is less repression.

Physically, the baths are divided into two parts. One is a public area which may be a steam room or simply a very large enclosed chamber, sometimes referred to by the clientele as an "orgy room." In these public rooms sexual contact can be made or group sexual activity may occur. The second main area of the baths is the individual room, which is assigned to the client as he enters the establishment. Its main features are a bed and a door with a lock on it. These private rooms exist primarily for the purpose of sexual activity, although clients often sleep there between sexual escapades. One way in which the individual homosexual can make sexual contact is by leaving the door of his room slightly ajar. His preference for a particular type of sexual activity may be indicated by the position in which he lies on the bed while the door remains ajar. If he lies on his back it may indicate he prefers to be fellated; if he lies on his side or sits on the bed then it is not clear what his preference is; if he lies on his stomach, the chances are high that he wishes to take the receptor role in anal intercourse.

As in the streets and parks, the encounters in the baths tend to be completely focused on sexual activity without much attempt at socialization, although this does occasionally occur. One of the remarkable features of the baths is the really very great amount of sexual contact that a man can have during a single visit to the bath. In fact, many customers are disappointed if they go to the baths and have only one sexual experience, even though they may feel it is satisfactory. I once interviewed a young man who preferred to take the receptor role in anal intercourse and had 48 sexual contacts in one evening, simply by going into his room, leaving the door open, lying down on his belly and letting 48 men in succession sodomize him. Just as a matter of note, it should be remarked that this young man had been married and was the father of two children.

In the baths one will see customers roaming around the halls, looking into rooms, and observing those that they meet in the halls. Like the gay bar, the bath is a sexual marketplace and one is judged by one's physical attributes. The baths as a social system are only possible because of the strong tendency to sexual promiscuity among male homosexuals, and it is simply not conceivable that lesbians, for example, would ever be able to develop such an institution. Just why there is this marked discrepancy in the promiscuity rate between male and female homosexuals is a fascinating subject which we shall defer to a later part of the discussion.

Jack is a 32-year-old insurance broker who is a frequent customer of the baths. He is married and has three children and lives in many ways a completely conventional suburban life. He tells his wife that he likes to go out on Friday nights with the boys, and she has no real reason to question this, since there has never been any question of adultery during the six years that they have been married. He checks into the baths around 10:30 and stays there until about 3:00 A.M., during which time he has numerous sexual encounters. He goes there purely for the sex and has no interest in having any social contact with any of the people in the baths other than the most casual of conversations. He does not reveal his identity in any way. He signs the enrollment book with a false name and address. One of the advantages of the baths, of course, is the almost complete anonymity which they offer. The client is not dressed nor does he have to take his sexual partner back to his own hotel or apartment and, in fact, does not really have to engage him in much conversation. Such a setup is a perfect one for a respectable married man, such as Jack, who wishes to have some homosexual satisfaction without becoming involved in the social and interpersonal aspects of the homosexual community. He will usually get his room assignment and then walk around the halls a bit to see if he can find anyone he likes. He then goes to the "orgy room," where he engages in a certain amount of reciprocal oral-genital activity. There is actually very little anal activity in the "orgy room"; fellatio is the main kind of sexual practice there. After he tires of this he will cruise the halls until he sees a room in which there is somebody to whom he is sexually attracted. He goes in and has sex. This may happen once or twice. When he feels sexually gratified, he will leave the baths and go home. In most other aspects of his life, Jack seems to be quite the normal husband and father and says that he has a reasonably satisfactory sexual relationship with his wife. He finds homosexual sex, however, more exciting, but does not feel that it in any way detracts from the meaningfulness of his marital relationship. When he is asked if he is worried whether he will run into anyone he knows from the baths, he says that sometimes this bothers him a little bit, but then he realizes that if they are there, then they are homosexuals too, and he has really nothing to fear. In the city in which he lives the baths are considered quite safe and there have not been any police raids, although this is not true of a number of major cities in the country.

If one were called upon to justify the existence of the homosexual baths, this would not be too difficult a task, since they are basically only known to those who are already homosexually oriented, and provide no nuisance to the public. If anything, they keep homosexuals out of those public places where they most frequently run into trouble with the police. The almost exclusive focus there on genital activity in preference to any other kind of relationship that might take place between two persons is, of course, not one which can evoke much enthusiasm from anyone who feels that sexual activity should be integrated into a meaningful human relationship. Nevertheless, it is difficult to see how the baths do any harm, since their clientele have already reached the stage which perhaps could be best described as a concentration upon sexual activity for its own sake.

The Gay Bar

The gay bar has almost become a social institution in America. It is the central public place around which gay life revolves and is to be found in all large and medium-sized cities across the country. We would like to describe here the "typical gay bar," although, of course, there is no such thing, any more than there is a "typical straight bar." Perhaps, narrowing our focus a bit, what we want to describe is what I call the "middle-class" gay bar, by which I mean not that all its members are necessarily middle-class socioeconomically, but rather that middle-class proprieties are observed and that there is nothing unique or specialized about the bar. We will not, for example, be concerned with the leather-jacket motorcycle bars, nor with the hustler bars so beautifully described by Rechy, nor with those bars which provide entertainment such as drag shows and male go-go dancers.

Perhaps the most important fact about a gay bar is that it is a sexual marketplace. That is, men go there for the purpose of seeking sexual partners, and if this function were not served by the bar there would be no gay bars, for, although homosexuals also go there to drink and socialize, the search for sexual experience is in some sense the core of the interaction in the bar. It should, however, be obvious that there must be more going on in the bar than simply people meeting and leaving; otherwise the bar could not exist as a commercial enterprise. People have to come there for a time long enough to drink, in order to make it profitable to the management to run these bars. And gay bars are very profitable and have sprung up in large numbers. It is estimated that there are about 60 gay bars in Los Angeles and about 40 in San Francisco. A number of heterosexuals have converted their own taverns into gay bars simply because they have found it more profitable to run a gay bar, even though they are sometimes not particularly delighted with the clientele. The gay bar plays a central role in the life of very many homosexuals—one which is much more important than the role played by straight bars in the life of all but a few heterosexuals. This is connected intimately with the use of the gay bar as a sexual marketplace and, of course, with the fact that homosexuals, as homosexuals, have really no place else where they can congregate without disclosing to the straight world that they are homosexual.

What does a gay bar look like? In the first place, unlike most middle-class straight bars, it is almost exclusively populated by males. Sometimes non-homosexuals accidentally walk into a gay bar and it is usually this lack of women that makes them aware that they may have inadvertently walked into a homosexual setting. There are a few bars in which lesbians congregate along with male homosexuals, especially in cities which are not large enough to support a lesbian bar. But even in the larger cities, lesbian bars are not very common. They are never as large as the large metropolitan male gay bars. This is because female homosexuals are much less promiscuous than male homosexuals and really not able to support a sexual marketplace on the scale that males do.

Occasionally, "fruit flies," i.e., women who like to associate with male homosexuals, are found in gay bars, although they are not a very prominent part of any gay bar scene. Why a woman who is not a lesbian would like to associate with male homosexuals is a question which cannot be altogether answered in general, except to say that some of these women obviously find homosexual men a lot less threatening than heterosexual men, since the former are not interested in them sexually. Since these women are not potential sexual partners for the males, they are not potential sources of rejection for them either, and thereby they find themselves the subject of much attention by the male clientele. Consequently, they are the beneficiaries of a great deal of sociability without being objects of seduction. Some women find this a very appealing position.

In the gay world there is a tremendous accent on youth and this is reflected in the composition of the bar clientele.

Youth is very much at a premium and young men will go to the bars as soon as they have passed the legal age limit. This varies from state to state; it is 18 in New York and 21 in California. Along with the younger men, there are somewhat older men who are trying to look young. They attempt to accomplish this primarily by dress. The typical bar costume is the same style of dress that an average college undergraduate might wear. It would consist of a sport shirt, Levis, and loafers or sneakers. In this "typical" middle-class gay bar which I am attempting to describe, extremely effeminate dress and mannerisms are not well tolerated. Nevertheless, it would not be correct to say that the scene in a gay bar looks like a fraternity stag party. There is a tendency toward effeminacy in the overall impression one gets from observing the bar, although this may not necessarily be anything striking or flagrant. There is a certain softness or absence of stereotypical masculine aggression present in the conversations and behavior of the bar patrons. Also, in spite of the fact that the modal bar costume is very much like that one would see on a college campus, there is a good deal of special attention paid by the bar patrons to their dress, so that they seem almost extraordinarily well groomed. There is thus a feeling of fastidiousness about the appearance of the young men in the bar which, along with their muted demeanor, rather clearly differentiates the overall *Gestalt* of the gay bar from that which would be experienced upon entering a gathering of young male heterosexuals. There are usually a few clearly identifiable homosexuals, although the majority of individuals in the bar are not identifiable and would not be thought homosexual in another setting. It seems to be the general consensus of gay bar observers that fights are less likely to break out in a gay than in a straight bar. This is, I think, probably attributable to the psychological characteris-

tics of the clientele rather than to anything about the structure of the bar itself. Male homosexuals would certainly
rather make love than war.

One of the clearest differences between the gay and the
straight bar is that in the gay bar the attention of the patrons
is focused directly on each other. In a gay bar, for example,
the patrons who are sitting at the bar itself usually face away
from the bar and look toward the other people in the room
and toward the door. When a new patron walks in, he receives a good deal of scrutiny, and people engaged in conversation with each other just naturally assume that their
interlocutors will turn away from them to watch each new
entering patron. All this is, of course, part of the pervasive
looking and cruising which goes on in the bar.

There is a great deal of milling about in the bar and individuals tend to engage in short, superficial conversations
with each other. They try to make the circuit around the bar
to see everyone in it, perhaps stopping to chat with their
friends but usually not for very long. In a way, the shortness
and superficiality of the conversations in the bar mirror that
same brevity and shallowness of interpersonal relations which
characterize gay life as a whole.

Heterosexual observers and even homosexuals who are not
habitués of the bar scene often express great perplexity about
the bars—they cannot quite understand what's going on
there. They seem to be bewildered by the sight of all these
young men standing around and communicating so little with
one another. The patrons stand along the walls, it seems, for
hours, without speaking. They move around the room and
talk at length with almost no one. One heterosexual observer
said that he felt as if everyone in the room were standing
around waiting for some important figure to come in, but
of course he never comes. He likened the scene to a reception
for a foreign ambassador, where everyone stands around

simply marking time until the dignitary arrives. In a sense, this observer was correct, for the young men *are* waiting for some important person to arrive, one who will never arrive— but it is not a foreign ambassador. Each is waiting for a handsome young prince to come and carry him off in his arms. They're waiting for the ideal sexual object, and if they don't find him they may very well go home alone, in spite of the fact that there are sometimes hundreds of other attractive young men right there in the bar.

The gay bar, then, in a sense may be thought of as a stage on which is played out a fantasy in which the hero never arrives. The reason why heterosexuals and even some homosexuals cannot understand what is going on is because they are not a party to this fantasy. They imagine that if you are going to a place to seek a sexual partner, you go in, look around a little bit, walk up to somebody that you like, engage in a conversation, and then go out together. And sometimes this is precisely what does occur in the gay bar. Very often, in fact. But the bewildering problem which confronts the uninitiated observer is why this does not happen more often; why, in fact, all these good-looking and well-dressed young men are standing around uncommunicative.

Sherri Cavan (1966, p. 192) has made the suggestion that in the homosexual pickup bar it may happen that encounters are never begun because each party is waiting for the other to offer the first words of greeting. This is presumably due to the fact that when the situation involves two males, it is not clear who is expected to make the initial overture. One cannot deny the saliency of this observation. Nevertheless, I do not think it alone accounts fully for the strange situation in the gay bar, since one would expect the reverse to occur just as well, i.e., since both parties can make the initial overture, one would think that at least one of the members of the hypothetical pair could overcome his shyness. I think the sociological explanation fails to take into account the psychological factors involved. As many observers have noted, homosexuals are very much afraid of rejection, and hence, have an inordinate hesitancy about making an approach. I think this is due to the following reason: the only aspect of their self which male homosexuals are able to adequately present in a bar situation is their physical appearance. If they are rejected in making a conversational opening, this is interpreted (probably correctly) to mean a rejection of that crucial part of themselves, namely, their desirability as a sexual partner. Hence, their self-esteem is very much at stake and they have a great deal to lose by being rejected.

It must be remembered that in the gay world the only real criterion of value is physical attractiveness; consequently, a rejection by a desired partner is a rejection of the only valued part of one's identity in that world. When we understand this, I think we understand why the fear of rejection is so prevalent among homosexual men.

The gay bar, is, then, a lot less licentious than people who are not aware of what is going on there might be inclined to think. When heterosexual men enter a gay bar for the first time for the purpose of simply visiting it, they often seem afraid that somehow they will be rapidly approached, or perhaps even attacked, by the sexual deviants present inside the bar. This, of course, is about as far from reality as it is possible to imagine. It would not be unusual if none of the patrons would engage them in conversation during the entire course of the evening. If they are not young and handsome, they may well have great difficulty in communicating with anyone after even a great deal of effort on their part.

A word should be said, I suppose, about the function of the gay bar as a source of group solidarity and as a place where one can meet one's friends and exchange gossip. I think, however, that this function is obvious and that it need not be elaborated upon. Many homosexuals frequent gay bars for reasons other than seeking sexual partners. If sex eventuates from the bar interaction, this is fine, but it is not the reason they went there in the first place. They went there for sociability. And yet this too must be qualified, for in the back of their minds is usually the thought that perhaps that special person will walk through the door tonight and they will meet him and go home with him.

The "cosmetic" quality of the gay bar is a result, in large part, of the need for anonymity which pervades all the public places of the gay world. If one can only present the visible and non-identifying aspect of one's identity, one's physical appearance will be the central aspect that can be displayed to others. If homosexuals could meet *as homosexuals* in the kinds of social settings in which heterosexuals can (e.g., at school, at work) where the emphasis on finding sexual partners is not the controlling force behind all the social interaction which transpires, a great deal of the anonymous promiscuity which now characterizes homosexual encounters would be replaced by a more "normal" kind of meeting between two persons. Perhaps, then, the sexual relationships which develop would become more stable. Maybe the gay bar itself would not change—this can only be a matter for conjecture—but, at any rate, it would not be so central to gay life.

Choosing a Locale for Sexual Liaisons

I shall conclude this chapter on public places with a few comments about the comparative merits of the various homosexual public places as regards their value as sexual marketplaces. I think in this regard the great divide would be between the bar, on the one hand, and the baths, street, parks, and rest rooms, on the other. The latter places are much more suitable for those homosexuals whose immediate interest is focused upon genital contact and who will not go to the bars because they don't wish to stand around for several hours in the hope that they might possibly meet a sexual partner. They know that if they go to the baths, for example, they will almost certainly find one, if not many. However, the streets, parks, and rest rooms have two clear advantages over the baths for such an individual. First, there is not much immediate competition for the sexual partner. Homosexuals who go there generally run into the other person alone and thus, in the eyes of the cruiser, the desired sexual partner will probably have to take him unless he wants to wait an undetermined amount of time for another person to come along. Second, there is an admission charge, in the range of three to six dollars (depending upon time of day and day of the week), to the baths, whereas the parks, streets, and rest rooms are free (providing, of course, one does not get arrested, in which case the evening's diversion may be very expensive indeed). Furthermore, in none of the places except the bar are there the distractions of conversation, alcohol, music, and sometimes even dancing or entertainment. Excluding the bars, public places are used almost exclusively by homosexuals for explicit sexual purposes. The advantage of the bar, of course, is that it provides a chance for a conversation with a potential partner before the sexual contract is made. Thus, individuals who are concerned about the psychological characteristics of their partners have a chance to find out something about them. Also, of course, this lends a great aura of respectability to the whole affair, whereas simply meeting for a sexual encounter in a rest room is, in our society, quite clearly defined as disreputable.

It is interesting that the specification of the sexual act(s) to occur is not part of a contract for a sexual encounter; that is, individuals who meet in a bar or in a park and then adjourn to one of their apartments do not usually discuss what kind of sexual behavior is going to take place. I think this can be accounted for by the fact that male homosexuals are quite able to vary their sexual performance so as to find some satisfactory *modus operandi* in bed. While they might not find a partner who likes to do what they find most enjoyable sexually, the chances are very high that they will be able to find some kind of sexual behavior which is mutually satisfactory, at least to some extent. Occasionally, of course, this does not happen and one hears, every so often, stories told in the form of gossip about the time the individual met someone, went home with him, and they both found out that they wished to take precisely the identical role and that they were looking for someone to take a reciprocal role and this could not be done. This is, however, not a very common happening. One thing is clear, and that is that it is not very predictable from the physical appearance and mannerisms of the potential partner just what he will or will not do in bed. In extreme cases of effeminacy one can usually predict that the individual will take a receptor role with regard to his partner's penis, but aside from this, predictability is poor. The only other exception is the hustler, who classically only takes the insertor role, feeling that this is consistent with his image (either to himself and/or to his partner) of his "real" heterosexuality.

This might be an appropriate place to introduce the term "fetishization." Marx spoke of the fetishism of commodities, meaning that in industrial society individuals were bemused by the plethora of material goods and so they sacrificed a rich, non-alienated existence to perform alienated work, in order to be able to obtain material goods. Happiness is to be achieved by the acquisition of automobiles, clothes, homes, televisions, etc. Psychiatrists, on the other hand, speak of fetishism in connection with a particular kind of sexual perversion in which the individual is sexually excited only by either a part of his sexual partner's body—for example, the foot—or by a non-human object which has some connection with sexuality, such as a shoe or other piece of clothing.

Both the Marxian and the psychiatric notions of fetishization have in common the idea of a narrowing down of one's range of action from a rich or a full existential encounter, to a narrow, segmented area of experience. The purpose of this narrowing is that it enables the individual to gain some control and sense of efficacy in the interaction. In the case of commodity fetishism, this is the only meaningful activity in which industrial man can engage, since his work is alienated. The acquisition of commodities, then, becomes something which is to him the source of meaning in life. In sex fetishism, the individual, because of psychological problems, is unable to relate to the sexual partner as a total human being and relates only to a part of the body or to a piece of clothing.

As has been pointed out by the Russian philosopher Vladimir Soloviev, if a man relates to a woman only as a sexual object, e.g., only as a vagina, this is a form of fetishization. I think, then, it will be very clear to the reader that the public places of gay life are based on and, at the same time, encourage sex fetishization of a most dehumanizing kind. The focus in some of the public places is on a very brief sexual encounter, measured in terms of minutes, which occurs often under the most degrading circumstances. The gay bar tends to encourage the "one-night stand." This is sex without obligation or commitment, without significant personal encounter, sex for the sake of sex alone. It cannot be denied that long-term relationships do result from encounters in bars and even, to a minor extent, in the other public places, but these are more the exception than the rule, and these more significant relationships can certainly not be expected as a result of a visit to one of these places— or, for that matter, by repeated visits to such places. The individual who frequents the public places soon learns not to expect any more than a brief sexual experience. He looks to the public places for sex and must look elsewhere for the remaining meaning around which he can center his life. It is not difficult, I think, to see that such fragmentation of sex from the rest of one's human world is not conducive to personal happiness or good social adjustment.

4

Ten Hours

On a Saturday afternoon, remarkable by the absence of fog in San Francisco, I went to visit Paul, who is a social science professor at a Bay Area college. I arrived at 2:00 in the afternoon and stayed with him until midnight, at which time I left the party to which we had gone.

Paul

Paul lived in the top flat of an old, refurbished Victorian mansion—very typically San Franciscan—where he had resided for the past six years. At the time I visited with him he was living alone. Paul was 37 years old. He was exclusively homosexual and had been involved in homosexual activities and in the gay world for about 20 years. He had been born and raised in Boston and did all his college and graduate work in the East. He came to San Francisco to take an academic post when he was in his early 30's, and had lived in his present apartment all this time. His homosexual experiences began with some of his high school chums when he was a senior and had continued until the present time. One of the interesting aspects of his sexual preference is that he has always preferred partners of the same age that he was when he came out. I am unable to say, on the basis of the evidence I have from interviewing him, just what psychological factors may have determined this particular preference. It is certainly clear, however, that he does not feel particularly attracted to men his own age, although he has by no means restricted his sexual activity to males under 20.

As a matter of fact, Paul has had two "gay marriages" during his life, one lasting for about four months, the other for about nine months. The longer one occurred when he was 24 and was completing graduate work. The shorter affair occurred just a year before I met him.

Paul looks back with a great deal of nostalgia on these two affairs. While he is aware that they were difficult and, ultimately, had to be abandoned, he feels that they were in some ways the high points in his life, since the intimacy and companionship which he has been seeking were only realized during these times. His first affair was with a young man his own age who lived two blocks away. While the two men did not ever live together, they spent almost all their time together. The relationship was very intense for about five months, and neither of them had any outside sexual relations during this period. Gradually, however, they appeared to "lose interest" in restricting their sexual activities to their relationship and they both began having sex with other men. Although they had discussed this "infidelity" at great length and decided that it would be permissible and would not end their special relationship, they were unable to overcome the jealousy which the "extra-marital affairs" engendered. Finally, they decided it would be best for them to simply remain friends and give up any ideas that they were going to be together for the rest of their lives.

Paul's recent affair was with a 20-year-old college student who lived with him in his San Francisco apartment. Unlike the earlier affair, in which Paul met his partner at the university, he met this boy at a San Francisco bar. Paul has taken the wise decision not to have any sexual involvement with any of his students, and so he has to rely on gay bars as a meeting place for potential partners. When I asked him whether he could meet anybody through his gay friends, he said that this was not a very good way of meeting people, since while it would sometimes occur, most of his close gay friends were men of his own age who tended to prefer partners older than he did. Consequently, there were few young men in their late teens and early 20's whom he could meet through these individuals.

The relationship with Jim, his recent lover, was intense, stormy, and rather short-lived. It was a fairly typical homosexual affair in that it began with sexual contact on the first night. After the initial sexual encounter, Paul invited Jim to come and live with him. He feels now that he made a mistake in doing this, since Jim became financially dependent on him. Paul recognizes that this dependence was very bad for the relationship, because it caused Jim first to feel obligated and then resentful, and caused Paul to feel that perhaps the only reason Jim was interested in him was his money. Paul, who had lived alone for well over ten years, found living with a 20-year-old boy—albeit one who was very sexually attractive to him—rather psychologically taxing, since his established routine was interrupted, especially by Jim's friends, who tended to be both effeminate and irresponsible. Paul says Jim was not at all effeminate, but *was* somewhat irresponsible, and that Jim's attitude toward such things as keeping the house neat and clean, showing up for appointments on time, borrowing Paul's car, and the like, was less than desirable from Paul's point of view. Finally, it became evident to Paul that Jim was having sexual affairs on the side and he felt that the situation was not really tenable any longer, so he asked Jim to leave. He sees Jim once in a while in the bars and they exchange a few words, but there is really nothing much left to their relationship.

Paul talked a great deal about the problem of gay marriages and of the promiscuity and instability in the gay world. He said what he would really like would be to find a lover whom he could live with for the rest of his life, and who would move into the suburbs with him—something a few of his fortunate friends apparently have been able to do. Meanwhile, his social life is limited to his sexual partners with whom he has sex usually once, but occasionally three, four, or five times, and his friends, with whom he has a completely asexual social relation, which involves going to cocktail parties, to the opera, and to the beach. Actually, his closest personal relationship now is with a woman his own age who teaches in the same school as he. She is single, although heterosexual, but she knows about Paul's homosexuality. While Paul suspects that she might become interested in him romantically if he gave her any encouragement, he has made it clear to her that he is exclusively homosexual, so that the suggestion of their relationship becoming sexual has not come up. He generally sees her about twice a week and it is, in some ways, the warmest relationship in Paul's current life.

He has a fantasy that he may someday be forced by loneliness into marrying this woman, or someone like her, and settling down into an asexual marriage of convenience, but he certainly can't do that now, because of his continued sexual interest in young males. Furthermore, he feels that such a marriage would represent a defeat for him, since he still hopes (although he admits this hope is probably quite unrealistic) to find a lover of his own sex.

The Twinkie

Paul had told me that sometime during the afternoon Kenny, a boy whom he had been seeing lately, would possibly come over. Kenny, age 17, was what Paul calls a twinkie. This, he explained, is a sexually desirable young man who is still somewhat boyish, and this term he applies to the young males in their late teens and early 20's of whom he is especially fond. Paul said he has had a lot of trouble with Kenny because Kenny, like kids this age, tends to be irresponsible and when he says he is coming over, he very often does not; when he agrees to call, he frequently neglects to do so; and so on. Nevertheless, Kenny did show up in the late afternoon. He was a very engaging blond high school senior, whom Paul had met at one of the semi-gay coffee houses where homosexuals too young to enter the bars can go. Kenny's "line" was that he was really straight, but that he would engage in homosexual sex with someone he liked. Although Kenny was not, strictly speaking, a hustler, there *was* a financial element in his relation with Paul, since Paul would very often take him out, would spend money on him for dinner and shows, and would buy him presents.

The conversation we had with Kenny seemed to revolve

around Kenny's car and the troubles he was having with it, and his desire to travel around the world next year. Paul more or less went along with this kind of fantasy on Kenny's part, although it appeared to me that he looked on this sort of adolescent preoccupation as something he had to put up with for the pleasure of Kenny's company. Nevertheless, it was clear that Paul was quite good at putting up with it and engaging Kenny in this kind of 17-year-old dialogue. It has been apparent from my observations of other homosexual males who, like Paul, prefer sexual partners of Kenny's age that they often have a remarkable facility for being able to talk to these kids in their own language. This ability is, of course, not limited to homosexuals, for youth workers and other such professionals are also required to communicate in the language of the adolescent. But without it Paul would certainly be unable to engage Kenny or his peers in any kind of relationship other than a merely sexual one, which would then probably have to be based on the exchange of hard cash. This Paul would find distasteful because, while he sometimes patronizes hustlers, he does not particularly like to think that the only reason his partners are having sex with him is because of the money. He would rather allow himself to think that although these youngsters do like the money, they also really like *him* and that this is one of the reasons they go to bed with him. And in a sense, I think he is correct, because there certainly was a camaraderie between Paul and Kenny that went beyond the fact that Kenny got certain material benefits out of the relationship.

After a couple of hours, Kenny had to go home to have dinner. Paul and I decided to go out and have our dinner in one of San Francisco's gay restaurants. These are attached to bars and, like gay bars, are mostly patronized by males, except that sometimes one sees some lesbian couples or an occasional trio in which there is a female present. Paul didn't know anybody in the restaurant or in the bar, and so we didn't spend any length of time there. After dinner we went to visit Paul's friend Bill, a 27-year-old Negro who worked as a clerk in San Francisco's financial district.

Paul's relationship with Bill began with a one-night stand, but they did not again have sex together. Bill was living with a Caucasian boy two years younger than him in a sort of semi-roommate, semi-lover arrangement which had been going on for about six months. They occasionally slept together (approximately two or three times a month), but most of their sexual activity was outside the relationship. They did not consider themselves "married" and did not have any romantic notions about the relationship or its continuance. It seemed to me that this kind of relationship had a higher chance of lasting than one which was of the more romantic kind favored by Paul and so many of his homosexual friends. We sat around at Bill's and talked for a couple of hours about a lot of different things, including the gay scene, what was going on at the opera next season, and other miscellaneous gossip. Bill's roommate never did come in.

Homosexuality among Negroes

It is perhaps not inappropriate at this point to insert just a few observations about homosexuality among Negro males that I have encountered during my research. There presently exists no scientific study of homosexuality in the Negro community, and yet this phenomenon may well be of a quite different character than homosexuality among Caucasians. We do not even have any incidence figures, since Kinsey limited his study of American male homosexuality to whites.

As we shall see, one of the most popular current explanations for the origins of homosexual object-choice (i.e., sexual orientation) is the type of family constellation in which the homosexual-to-be is raised. The Negro family in America is often characterized by some of the features which are said to lead to homosexuality (i.e., domination by the mother, with a weak or absent father). We are thus led to wonder (assuming this familial explanation of homosexuality has some validity) just what factors prevent Negro males from showing a higher incidence of homosexuality than they do. (In the absence of evidence to the contrary, we are obliged not to assume that the incidence of homosexuality among Negroes is any different than it is among whites.) The influence of peers and of the Negro culture at large would, of course, be crucial factors in controlling the extent of homosexual behavior. Clearly, we know almost nothing about this very complex subject. I mention it to indicate the existence of an important area yet to be explored by social science, rather than to shed any light on it myself.

It is of interest to note that there is no all-Negro gay bar in the city of San Francisco, in spite of the fact that 10 percent of the population is Negro. The reason for this is very simple: if an all-Negro gay bar tried to develop, it would soon become integrated, because it would be invaded by white males who were looking for Negro partners. There is a significant percentage of white male homosexuals who prefer Negro partners and there are also not a few Negroes who prefer white partners, and thus there is an inevitable mixing of the races in gay bars. This is not true, of course, in those southern cities where bars are still segregated. But in San Francisco, which is a fairly integrated city, at least by American standards, an all-Negro gay bar does not exist. I am informed, however, by people who have been resident in New York and Chicago that in these larger cities, which have very extensive Negro ghettos, there do exist all-Negro gay bars.

I can say no more about this matter except to urge that a scientific study of homosexuality among Negroes be commenced. One of the factors which will, of course, have to be taken into consideration is the rapidly changing attitude of Negroes toward whites, in light of the increasing militancy of the Negro movement.

Interest in the Arts

As I indicated above, one of the areas to which Paul and Bill directed the discussion was the opera. My experience in conversations with homosexuals has been that they show an especial interest in the arts. Hooker (1957) notes the same phenomenon. There is more interest in and knowledge about opera, ballet, and theater in homosexual groups than I have noticed in heterosexual groups of comparable age and socioeconomic level. I also have observed that homosexuals are particularly attracted to professional careers in the arts, especially in the performing arts, and a number of other writers have noted that there seems to be an unusual percentage of homosexuals who have taken up acting as an occupation. In a very interesting recent article, Richard Green and John Money (1966) reported on a longitudinal study of 20 boys who had come to their attention because of symptoms of marked effeminacy which had begun prior to puberty. They found that in nine of the 20 boys there was also seen, prior to puberty, a striking capacity for role-taking and stage acting. This capacity occurred, therefore, well before the age at which these boys would show any strong sexual interest in their fellows, and certainly before the age at which they might find out that the world of acting offered a haven for individuals who did not want to conceal their homosexuality from the straight world. In other words, the data indicate that the high incidence of homosexuality in the theater is by no means due solely to a calculation on the part of homosexuals that this is a convenient occupation for them. It seems that their path toward acting begins at a time in life well prior to the time when they might make such a rational decision.

The explanation of this very interesting phenomenon is not entirely clear. It is possible that the boys are able to adopt an effeminate role because they *already* have a primary talent for role-taking. On the other hand, the primary factor may be effeminacy, in which case they may act and dress up as a girl in order to provide a socially acceptable outlet for their feminine characteristics. It seems most likely, however, that effeminate behavior in young boys is a response to subtle cues on the part of parents that such behavior is acceptable or even desirable. It may even represent the acting out of unconscious wishes on the part of the parent that the child be a girl. But since not every boy who is so pressured responds with effeminacy, there may well be a psychological trigger as well as a parental force that releases it. This trigger may be a personality trait or talent for role-playing. If this is true, then a propensity for a career in dramatic arts and a tendency toward effeminacy (and thus toward a particular type of homosexuality) may arise from the same source.

I don't mean to suggest by summarizing this study of Green and Money either that the majority of male homosexuals are effeminate or that the interest in the arts so characteristic of homosexual groups is derived from the same origins as an interest in acting as a career. Nevertheless, there are certain connections here which have been noted repeatedly by different observers and deserve thoughtful consideration. It is clear, at any rate, that there is very probably some early tendency toward an interest in those kinds of activity which lead to later interest in the arts and in acting. Such a tendency appears to exist well prior to puberty and therefore prior to the age at which sexual orientation becomes a conscious part of the homosexual's life.

A Party

At about 10:00 in the evening, Paul and Bill went to a party given in a fashionable suburb of San Francisco by a homosexual married pair. I was invited to go along and did so, staying until about midnight. One of the men who gave the party was in his 40's and was employed in the publishing world. The other was an accountant who worked in San Francisco. They had been married for about six years and their relationship seemed quite stable and was said by all to be fairly monogamous. The guests were all middle-class individuals, and included the following occupations: graduate student, physician, retail clerk, junior executive, hospital orderly, college undergraduate, chemist. I was not able to find out all the occupations of the guests; I should say that there were about 25 to 30 people there. One of the most interesting things about the party was that presents were passed out to all the guests and most of them were of a sexual nature: these included tubes of KY Jelly (used in anal intercourse), pictures of nude and semi-nude young males, copies of Henry Miller novels, an address book with humorous inscriptions of a sexual nature, and a book of some drawings depicting sexual activity. The conversations throughout the entire evening were permeated with homosexual jokes and references. This is not an atypical example of the behavior of middle-class adult homosexual men when in a homosexual setting. It is a good example, I think, of what I have called sex fetishism. There was, however, no overt sexual behavior at all during the party and no couples adjourned to the bedrooms. Some later conversations with one or two of the participants revealed that probably two of the people there found new sexual partners that evening, but the overt activity was basically social rather than sexual in nature. Nevertheless, the social intercourse relied heavily on sexual innuendo for its vitality.

Certainly there are a number of factors which can explain this kind of behavior. One of them is clearly the "releaser" effect of a social situation which is defined as homosexual. These men are people who have to conceal their sexual preferences in their daily occupational activities. Thus, when they get together with each other socially, there is a tendency to "let their hair down" and assert the usually hidden homosexual aspect of their identity. There are perhaps two ways of looking at this situation. One is that the bringing together of a group of homosexuals *allows* them to express their otherwise suppressed homosexual feelings. The other interpretation is that bringing them together *encourages* them to talk about the one thing they clearly have in common, namely, their sexual preference. These two interpretations are, however, not mutually contradictory. It seems clear that they are both operative. Still, the overall effect on the observer is that there is a rather adolescent quality to the entire affair, which reminds one in a way of a high school fraternity stag party— although with quite different conversational content and mannerisms.

Gay Parties

I left this particular party at about midnight and said goodby to Paul and to some of the people I had met there. But since I have described this one type of gay party, perhaps it would be appropriate to say a few words about other types of parties. There certainly are such things as arranged orgies, where people are deliberately brought together by the host for the purpose of engaging in group sexual behavior. On the other hand, group sexual behavior at parties can arise without prearrangement. One of the interesting phenomena of gay life is the fact that, given the bar situation as we have discussed it in the preceding chapter, many young men are left standing around in the bar at closing time (2:00 A.M. in California). Consequently, they are faced with the problem of where to go. There are basically three kinds of places where they can go and still remain in contact with the organized gay community. First, they can go to the baths and participate in the sexual activity that goes on there. Second, they can go to one of the after-hours coffee houses, in which the interaction is very much like that which occurs in the gay bar, except that it drags on until 4:00 and 5:00 A.M. Third, they can go to an after-bar party, which is typically arranged on the spot by one of the patrons in the bar. Usually word of this is circulated around among the patrons, although I have heard it announced over the loudspeaker in a couple of the bars. There is a variable degree of selectivity in inviting guests to an after-bar party, but very often total strangers are invited. This is, of course, rather risky, since they might be police officers.

The character of after-bar parties varies considerably. To some extent, it is related to the character of the bar from which the party originates. If the party originates from a bar where the customers tend not to meet each other very easily, it is often characterized by the worst aspects of bar socializing. As one of my interviewees said, "Guys simply stand around or sit around, sometimes dancing a little, continuing to hope they will be approached by the young man of their dreams." On the other hand, parties which originate from bars that allow more physical contact in the bar itself are more likely to develop into locales for group sexual activity. Usually this activity is very similar to the kind that is found in the baths, i.e., one room where fellatio seems to be the predominant activity, and separate bedrooms where couples adjourn for the purpose of anal intercourse. Several of the after-bar parties I attended were raided by the police, but, humorously, not because the police suspected homosexual activities, but rather because the participants insisted upon playing the phonograph too loudly and the neighbors thought there was a wild fraternity party going on next door. The coming of the police marked the end of the parties that I attended, since the participants were quite upset by the intrusion and could not continue the festivities once their latent fears of arrest were aroused.

Sex Fetishism

Perhaps in closing this chapter, I might say another word about what I have called sex fetishism. It seems to me that the most striking thing about gay life in general, which differentiates it from the straight world, is that its participants devote an inordinate amount of time to sexual matters. This does not mean that they actually have more sex, measured in orgasms, than heterosexuals. Interestingly enough, Kinsey has found that they actually have *fewer* orgasms over time than heterosexual males (Kinsey, 1948, pp. 631–36). This is not difficult to explain, however. As a matter of fact, it is almost a corollary of the sexual promiscuity which characterizes gay life. For if homosexuals' sexual relationships are transitory, this means that the homosexual male has to be constantly on the lookout for new partners in order to find somebody to go to bed with. As George Bernard Shaw pointed out, "Marriage is the most licentious of institutions." In other words, an individual who is living with a sexual partner will have many more opportunities for sexual relations than one who has to go out into a public place and seek a new partner every time he wants to have sex.

The causal relationship between sexual promiscuity and constant preoccupation with sex is very difficult to disentangle. It is something like the chicken-and-egg paradox; for it is not clear whether this sexual preoccupation is the *result* of the lack of a stable sexual partner, itself caused by a more basic tendency toward promiscuity, or whether, on the other hand, the promiscuity flows from the constant preoccupation with finding new partners. In a later chapter we will discuss the problem of promiscuity at some length, and so I will leave the hypotheses explaining these phenomena for later. Nevertheless, it seems clear that from a strictly descriptive point of view, sexual promiscuity and sex fetishism, i.e., a preoccupation with sex, are two of the hallmarks of gay life in America, and serve to distinguish it as a whole from the life of the heterosexual. Obviously, there are many heterosexuals who are obsessed with sex and many of them are also promiscuous. But sex fetishism and promiscuity do not pervade the entire heterosexual world in the way that they appear to pervade the male homosexual community. Nor, for that matter, do they characterize the female homosexual world, and *this* interesting contrast is one which will provide us a crucial clue in explaining this very serious problem.

5

•○•

Homosexuals and the Law

One evening, while talking to a young man in a San Francisco gay bar, I heard him complain about some aspects of his life and then say, "Maybe I'll go to Chicago. Gay kids are legal in Illinois." He was referring to the fact that in 1961 the Illinois legislature removed the laws governing sexual relations between consenting adults in private from the statute books, but he was also expressing here a common misunderstanding, the notion that homosexuality *per se* is illegal. This is incorrect; nowhere is it against the law to be homosexual, to be sexually attracted to members of one's own sex. What is illegal are certain acts, and the law does not discriminate in regard to the sex of the individuals who perform these acts, which are illegal in both a homosexual and a heterosexual context. This is due to a combination of factors, one of them being the fact that the law traditionally does not prohibit states of mind, but only proscribes certain forms of behavior. Another reason for this seeming anomaly is the fact that the statutes themselves are very ill-defined. It is certainly not clear from reading them, and sometimes it is not even clear to appellate courts, just exactly what they prohibit. This is obviously a result of the great reticence of the law-making bodies and courts which have enacted and enforced these statutes to discuss openly the matter of homosexual acts. As Morris Ploscowe pointed out, judges are very uneasy when they have to deal with cases involving abnormal sexual behavior. One court wrote, "We regret that the importance of this question [whether oral-genital contact, fellatio, is a crime against nature] renders it necessary to soil the pages of our reports with a discussion of a subject so loathsome and disgusting as the one confronting us" (Ploscowe, 1962, p. 183). The statutes themselves share the same reticence to describe the actual acts which they are prohibiting. In many states they merely prohibit "the crime against nature with man or beast," or "sodomy with man or beast." In the following chapter we will discuss in some detail the phrase "crime against nature," for in order to understand this term properly it is necessary to examine the concept of nature itself. Here we wish to point out that these statutes, which derive from the time of Henry VIII, traditionally include only anal intercourse; they do not include oral-genital relations, either fellatio or cunnilingus. In prohibiting anal intercourse, the prohibition applies *equally to heterosexual and to homosexual acts*. Therefore, we have a curious paradox: the law which is supposed to prohibit homosexuality is in reality a law which prohibits only one kind of homosexual act and is written so that it covers a good deal of what goes on in the bedrooms of heterosexually married couples as well. Under this law, a man who performs anal intercourse with his wife is guilty of sodomy, whereas a homosexual pair in the next apartment who are performing mutual fellatio are not doing anything illegal.

As a result of these confusions, the court has not known quite what to do with oral-genital relations, and there have been a number of differing interpretations by various courts in different jurisdictions. Some courts have redefined the sodomy laws to include fellatio or cunnilingus, whereas others have explicitly stated that the statute cannot cover these acts. In 1897 a California court held that the sodomy statute did not include fellatio or cunnilingus; therefore a separate statute (California Penal Code, Section 288a) was enacted to outlaw oral copulation. It should be emphasized that this California statute prohibits heterosexual as well as homosexual oral-genital relations. This kind of legislative resolution of the problem has been adopted in a number of states.

The statutes against certain sexual acts do not, by any means, exhaust the laws which are used against homosexuals. There are a number of very vaguely worded misdemeanor statutes that can be used by the authorities against behavior occurring in public places, which account for the majority of arrests for homosexual behavior. In California, there are three main categories: outrageous conduct, lewd and lascivious behavior, and the vagrancy laws. An example of these is California Penal Code, Section 650½: "A person who willfully and wrongfully commits any act which seriously injures the person or property of another, or which seriously disturbs or endangers the public peace or health, or which

Hoffman 1968

openly outrages public decency . . . for which no other punishment is expressly prescribed by this code, is guilty of a misdemeanor." The vagrancy laws in the United States appear to be derivative from English laws which were originally enacted to keep farm workers at work on the land and therefore prohibited individuals from wandering about. These laws prohibiting wandering or vagrancy are so vague that they can cover a great deal of homosexual behavior in public places, providing the authorities wish to interpret them in this fashion. For example, homosexuals who cruise parks or rest rooms can be arrested under any number of statutes. If they are actually found committing a homosexual act, they can be arrested under the sodomy or oral copulation laws; if they are engaged in solicitation or in physical contact with the partner short of a sexual act, they can be arrested for outrageous conduct or lewd and lascivious behavior; and if they are merely loitering around a men's room in a manner which the police consider to be for the purpose of eventual homosexual contact, they might be arrested under the vagrancy laws.

An Encounter with the Police

Richard is a 35-year-old photographic equipment salesman who has the habit of visiting a well-known men's room in a public building not far from where he works. I interviewed him on the morning after he had been arrested. He said he was charged with indecent exposure. On the night of the arrest he said that he acted more aggressively in the men's room than he habitually does because, as he said, "I was unusually horny." He stayed in the john for 30 to 35 minutes. One of the men in the room was masturbating, but Richard

was not interested in him because he did not find him sufficiently attractive. He went into one of the booths and was
sexually excited by the sight of the foot and pants leg of the
person in the stall next to him. This individual, whom he
imagined was an attractive young man, was wearing Levis and
tennis sneakers. He tried to attract him by foot-tapping, but
did not seem to be able to get a response. Finally, he got up
and went to the area near the urinals where he exposed his
genitals to a young man who had just walked through the
door. This did not bring any sign of sexual interest from the
man, so Richard finally became discouraged and left the
men's room. As soon as he walked out the door he was
arrested by the individual to whom he had exposed himself,
who was a police officer. Another individual, whom he had
seen leaving the john at the time he originally came in—at
least half an hour before—turned out to be the officer's associate.

This pattern of behavior is typical of that in which many
homosexuals engage. Obviously, it is quite risky, and especially
in view of the fact that Richard and his fellow john-cruisers
usually have sex *right in the lavatory* after they make a successful contact, it is no surprise that a number of them run
into legal trouble as a result of these practices. What is sur-
prising, rather, is that many of them apparently engage in
these practices for years *without* an arrest.

A Study of Homosexual Law Enforcement

My own observations about the relationships between
homosexuals and the law have been based on my interviews
of individuals who have generally not had any difficulty with
the law. Thus, while I had some general impressions about

the problem, I was not able to support these with what might be regarded as sufficient empirical data. Fortunately, however, a very excellent study done by the staff of the U.C.L.A. *Law Review* was published in March, 1966, entitled *The Consenting Adult Homosexual and the Law: An Empirical Study of Enforcement and Administration in Los Angeles County*. Their documented conclusions fully support my own general observations on the problem. Since this report is a somewhat technical study of approximately 200 pages, it is not, I think, beside the point to make a brief summary of some of the more important findings here.

The most widely used provisions for punishing homosexuals are in the disorderly conduct statute, which is Section 647 of the California Penal Code: "Every person who commits any of the following acts shall be guilty of disorderly conduct, a misdemeanor: (a) Who solicits anyone to engage in or who in any public place or in any place open to the public or exposed to public view engages in lewd or dissolute conduct. . . . (d) Who loiters in or about any toilet open to the public for the purpose of engaging in or soliciting any lewd or lascivious or any unlawful act."

This law was enacted in 1961 after the California legislature repealed the old Section 647 which defined vagrancy. This was the result of many years of criticism directed at the old statute for being much too vague, not requiring proof of any criminal act, and providing the possibility that a conviction could be based on events which happened some time before the arrest was made. According to interviews with 15 law enforcement agencies in the Los Angeles area, it appears that approximately 90 to 95 percent of all homosexual arrests are for violations of California Penal Code, Section 647(a). Of perhaps even greater interest is that the large majority of these arrests result from solicitation of decoys by homosexuals.

What are decoys? Decoys are law enforcement officers who intentionally provide homosexuals with the opportunity to make a proscribed solicitation. They are, very often, young and attractive and dress in the kind of clothing which would appeal to the homosexual male, such as tight-fitting Levis. They usually work with a fellow officer who keeps out of sight, but appears on the scene when the arrest is made.

Most convictions under 647(a) are based exclusively on the arresting officer's allegation that the defendant has made an oral solicitation for a lewd act. Usually the decoy's partner cannot get close enough to witness either the solicitation or the occasionally lewd touching.

Homosexuals frequently accuse the police of engaging in "entrapment." Actually, in the use of decoys the law makes a fine distinction between entrapment and "enticement." The distinction hinges on whether the intent to commit the crime originated in the mind of the defendant or in the mind of the officer. If the defendant has a pre-existing criminal intent, the officer's intent is irrelevant and there is no entrapment. It is permissible to entice the suspect who is engaged in criminal activity or who has a predisposition to commit the crime. Illegal inducement occurs only when it would be sufficient to lead the innocent into a criminal act.

There are really two issues involved here. The first is: do the police sometimes, or often, engage in behavior which actually constitutes illegal entrapment? For example, do they lead the defendant on by conversation which cannot be documented in court and in which the ultimate legal disposition revolves around the defendant's word against the officer's? The second question is: even if police were *never* to engage in any illegal entrapment devices, is it desirable that police manpower be used for this kind of activity? The first question is an empirical one, and a good deal of debate can be generated by asking homosexuals and police agencies to state their differing views on the subject. Police agencies maintain that their officers are well trained to avoid entrapment, and homosexuals claim that the police, in fact, do entrap them all the time. Since I have no evidence on this matter and the U.C.L.A. study presents none, I shall leave it here, except to point out that the answer to question number one hinges in part on our attitude toward question number two. This is because, obviously, abuses occur in any social system and, thus, in any law enforcement system. Hence police, when on actual duty and regardless of their training, sometimes do things which they are not supposed to do. Consequently, if their work depends on a very fine distinction between entrapment and enticement, it is to be expected that on some occasions they overstep the bounds. The question then becomes: is the behavior which they are out to stop of such a nature that it requires (a) the manpower involved in order to apprehend the offenders, and (b) the loss of individual rights which might occur if law enforcement officers are overzealous and overstep the strict legal criteria which are supposed to govern their activity? On this matter, let me quote from the conclusions and recommendations of the U.C.L.A. *Law Review* study:

> Empirical data indicate that utilization of police manpower for decoy enforcement is not justified. Societal interests are infringed only when a solicitation to engage in a homosexual act creates a reasonable risk of offending public decency. The incidence of such solicitations is statistically insignificant. The majority of homosexual solicitations are made only if the other individual appears responsive and are ordinarily accomplished by quiet conversation and the use of gestures and signals having significance only to other homosexuals. Such unobtrusive solicitations do not involve an element of public outrage. The rare indiscriminate solicitations of the general public do not justify the commitment of police resources to suppress such behavior.

It is accordingly recommended that operation of suspected homosexuals by police decoys be eliminated and that routine patrol of bars, public toilets and parks by plainclothes and uniformed officers be utilized to suppress offensive homosexual conduct. (Pp. 795–96.)

I need only add that I am in complete agreement with the conclusions as stated. As a matter of fact, I would argue further that putting out as decoys police officers who are young, attractive, and seductively dressed, and who engage in enticing conversations with homosexuals, is itself an outrage to public decency. Since practically no homosexual arrests involve complaints from anyone, it is a very good question just why public funds are being expended for this purpose.

Location of Arrests

It is very clear from interviewing homosexuals that there is no real fear that they will be arrested for sexual behavior occurring in the privacy of their own homes. Those men in my sample who have been arrested have all been arrested in public places. The U.C.L.A. study found that of their 493 felony arrest cases, only 24 acts took place in a private residence. All others were in public or semi-public places. Two hundred seventy-four were in rest rooms, 108 were in cars, 18 in jails, 17 in parks, 15 in the baths, and 11 on the beach. Of the 475 misdemeanor arrests, only six occurred in private locales (homes, hotels, apartments). One hundred thirty-nine were in rest rooms, 98 were in cars, 83 in parks, 62 in theaters, 49 in bars, 14 in streets, and five in the baths (pp. 707–8). It is virtually impossible to arrest individuals for private homosexual activity without exceeding the search-

and-seizure limitations. Thus there is no real attempt made to enforce against sexual relations between consenting adults in private.

It is very interesting in this regard to note that of the 493 felony arrests, 457 were for oral copulation. This is clearly because oral copulation is much the preferred activity in the kind of public place that would be visited by the police, particularly rest rooms, parks, theaters, and automobiles. Participants in anal intercourse usually want to engage in this activity where a bed is available, and thus they usually adjourn to private quarters. Fellatio, however, can occur without too much mechanical difficulty in any number of public places, such as the stall in a public toilet, the back of a movie theater, or in a park where one of the participants is standing up against a tree.

Homosexuals sometimes allege that police officers will arrest them and then either make a deal with the homosexual in which he has the choice of either orally copulating the officer or being arrested, or, more diabolically, will entice the homosexual into orally copulating him before revealing his identity, and then will arrest him anyway. This cannot, in general, be documented, but it is interesting to note that in 1927, in the case of People vs. Spaulding (81 Cal. App. 615, 254 Pac. 614), a conviction for oral copulation was affirmed, even though one of the arresting officers allowed himself to be orally copulated by the defendant before the arrest was made. Hence there is evidence that abuses do occur. However, the question is not really whether we can stop abuses by more efficient administration by law enforcement agencies, but, rather, whether the present system of decoy operation is basically justifiable. I think it is not.

While I agree with the recommendations of the U.C.L.A. *Law Review* on the subject of decoys, I do not question the necessity for patrolling of public places by uniformed police officers. Public sexual activity—both homosexual and heterosexual—in which there is very heavy petting, or genital display or contact, is simply too offensive to too many people to be permitted. There is no question that there are many homosexuals who engage in overt sexual behavior in public places. As a matter of fact, some of them will admit that they do so *because* the fact that they might be arrested is itself sexually exciting to them. There is simply no way of preventing these individuals from engaging in activity that would, under any circumstances conceivable at the present time, outrage passers-by. Hence it seems to me that the police cannot be blamed when an individual who has been caught sucking the penis of another man in a park or public lavatory finds himself in court. I have interviewed a sufficient number of adult male homosexuals who are highly intelligent and occupy respectable and even prestigious occupational positions to assert that a substantial portion of these men—though not the majority—cruise johns and parks and engage in sexual acts *in* the johns and parks. Thus, some kind of police surveillance of these public places would appear to be necessary.

The Homosexual in Court

After talking with homosexuals who have found their way into the arms of the law and after looking over the results of the Los Angeles study, I have the distinct impression that the participants in the courtroom drama, both the judge and the defendant, and in very many cases the prosecutor also, are all somewhat embarrassed by the whole affair and wish to get it over with as quickly as possible. Of the 493 felony arrests in the Los Angeles study, only 11 of the defendants asked for a jury trial. Clearly, the main desire of the defendant is to avoid publicity. This is very important to note, because the fact is that knowledge in the community that one is homosexual is much more damaging to a man's life than any sentence which is likely to be imposed by the court.

But what about the incredibly long prison sentences for sodomy that are written down in the statute books? Isn't it true that it is possible to get 10 or 15 years for a single homosexual act? Of course, it is *possible*, and these figures do appear in the statutes, but the Los Angeles study shows in very clear terms that this is not the kind of thing that happens. A comparison of the sentences imposed in the felony cases and in the misdemeanor cases shows quite similar outcomes. The defendant is fined, is given a jail sentence which is then immediately suspended, and is placed on probation. As a result of the 457 felony convictions, only three men went to prison. Furthermore, over 95 percent of the felony convictions are converted to misdemeanors by judicial action. This is possible in California because the judge can convert a conviction for oral copulation (though not for anal intercourse) from the status of a felony to a misdemeanor. As we noted, 457 of the 493 felony arrests were for oral copulation.

Hence, the likelihood of an individual who is arrested for a homosexual act going to prison is very low. What the defendant is really afraid of is that the people in the community will find out about his sexual proclivity, and it is this rather than the fear of legal penalties which makes him most upset when he is arrested. Probably he would prefer to have been arrested for income-tax evasion. So in this sense there is an analogy between present times and those times past when judges did not soil the court records with discussions of abominations against nature. The difference is that today, as Ploscowe noted from his own interviews, judges agree that homosexuality is not really deterrable. There are approximately 6,000,000 acts for every 20 convictions. The judges continue to feel that the *public* acts can be reduced by legal sanctions. Yet their feelings about middle-class men who are arrested in public places seem to be not generally indignation or a wish to punish, but rather, "Why did an intelligent man do a crazy thing like this?" The trials are handled without publicity, with great dispatch, and the sentences are very much lighter than a reading of the statute books would lead one to believe. Hardly anyone goes to prison. The judges realize that putting a homosexual into prison is like trying to cure obesity by incarceration in a candy shop. We know that there is a great deal of homosexual behavior in prison and that the incidence is much higher than in the general population, since prisons are by definition one sexed environments. Also, insofar as the judges have adopted a psychiatric view of homosexuality they feel that the men they see before them are mentally ill and that no purpose would be served by sending them to prison. The only reason, then, for sending a man to prison would be if he is a danger to the community, and the consenting adult homosexual is clearly no danger to anyone.

Registration of Homosexuals

In the State of California, any person convicted of anal intercourse, oral copulation, soliciting or engaging in lewd conduct, loitering to engage in or solicit lewd conduct, or indecent exposure must, within 30 days of his coming into the city or county in which he resides, register with the chief of police of the city, or the sheriff of the county. According to the Los Angeles study, law enforcement officials are very adamant in their desire to have homosexuals registered and are annoyed when the courts allow defendants to plead to a non-registerable lesser included offense. They say they favor registration because of their belief that homosexuals are prone to commit crimes against children and violent crimes (pp. 737–38).

It is a matter of empirical fact that the consenting adult homosexual who gets in trouble with the law is *not* prone to commit violent crimes or crimes against children. Homosexuals are no more prone to seduce young boys than are heterosexual males to seduce young girls. There is, indeed, an accent on youth in the male homosexual world, but this is hardly the same as pedophilia. The age of the male homosexual's ideal love object would be somewhere in the early 20's, but this is the same, after all, for heterosexual men, as a perusal of *Playboy* magazine will readily reveal. Those men who prefer young boys form a very special and distinct group, just as do those who prefer young girls, and they are a very small minority of the adult male population.

In 1965, the Institute for Sex Research at Indiana University (founded by the late Alfred C. Kinsey) published a massive volume on sex offenders (Gebhard *et al.*, 1965). Interviewers from the Institute personally talked with over 1,500 men convicted for a wide variety of sex offenses. It was necessary for them to subdivide their sample into various categories.

> On a priori grounds it is evident that for the majority of sex offenses there are three independent variables: (1) whether the offense involved a member of the same or opposite sex, i.e., whether the offense was homosexual or heterosexual in nature, (2) whether the sexual activity was consented to (consensual) or whether force or threat was involved, and (3) whether the object of the offense was a child, minor, or adult. (P. 11.)

The authors then go on to make a very significant statement, one which should forever dispose of the myth that homosexuals are prone to violence: "These three variables combine to form 12 types of sex offenses, which we reduced to nine because the use of force is rare in homosexual activity" (p. 11). The use of violence is thus seen to be a prerogative mainly of heterosexuals; it appears certain that homosexuals are actually *less* violent than heterosexuals. This point is worth emphasizing because a number of writers, with credentials that might indicate they ought to know better, have tried to promulgate the idea that homosexuals are unusually violent.

In this study, one of the categories in which offenders were classified was those who made homosexual overtures to, or had sexual contact with, boys under 12. If we examine the kind of sexual relations which went on between the two males involved, I think we can form a theory as to why force or violence would not be a factor. In 45 percent of the cases, masturbation was the technique, and in 38 percent of the cases, fellatio was performed on the boy. Anal intercourse occurred in only 4 percent of the cases. Masturbation or fellation of a boy involves producing an erection on his part and bringing him to orgasm. I think it is not difficult to see that this can only be done with the cooperation of the boy. In other words, these sexual techniques are not susceptible to force or violence. One cannot bring a boy to orgasm unless he is a consenting partner. Thus, while it is theoretically possible that there could be a category for homosexual offenses which would be analogous to heterosexual rape, this would only apply to anal intercourse, and this is not a technique which seems to be of very much interest to those homosexual adults who have sexual relations with boys under 12. The kind of thing that they want to do when they get the boy alone is something which is not possible to achieve by the use of compulsion.

Again, we should emphasize that those adult males who engage in sexual acts with young boys represent only a small fraction of the total adult male homosexual population. As a matter of fact, as the Kinsey Institute study pointed out, those individuals who were arrested for sexual offenses with boys under 12 are the least oriented toward their own sex of all males arrested for homosexual acts. They are generally bisexual; of those who had sex with boys under 12, ultimately nearly two-thirds will marry. Of those who had sexual relations with boys between the ages of 12 and 15 slightly more than half will marry. Of those men who had sexual relations with males over age 16, about 40 percent will ultimately marry. In other words, it is fair to say that the younger the male partner of the sex offender, the more likely he is to be bisexual *rather than exclusively homosexual.* As this study shows, most adult males who have sexual relations with boys under 12 also show a relative predisposition toward heterosexual offenses with girls under 16. "In brief, most of them are interested sexually in young people, preferably but not necessarily male, and their minimum age limit is quite elastic and can be stretched to suit the immediate circumstances" (Gebhard *et al.*, p. 272).

The point of this discussion is to show two things: first, because of the kind of sexual act they want to engage in, those adult males who have sexual relations with small boys would not be able to use force even if they wanted to, and there is no evidence that they want to. The second point is that the exclusive male homosexual is *not* the characteristic sex offender against children. He is much more likely to be a man who has been or will be married and who also has a tendency to want sex relations with young girls. The average adult male homosexual who goes to the gay bars or to the baths is no more likely to molest little boys than is the average male heterosexual likely to molest small girls. Hence the suggestion, made by police officials, that the consenting adult homosexual who is arrested is a potential danger to

·

children or is prone to violence is simply not true. While I do not wish to deny that there are indeed child molesters, it must be made clear that they are a separate class of persons and are not the men about whom this book is written.

Homosexual Law Reform

In 1955 the American Law Institute and in 1957 the English Committee on Homosexual Offenses and Prostitution (known as the Wolfenden Committee after its chairman, Sir John Wolfenden) both concluded that homosexual behavior between consenting adults in private should be removed from the jurisdiction of the criminal law. In 1961 the State of Illinois revised its entire penal code, and since the recommendation of the American Law Institute was embodied in that Institute's Model Penal Code, the Illinois legislature simply adopted the recommendation. This was done without significant public debate, in contrast to the procedure adopted in England where the recommendation of the Wolfenden Committee took ten years to finally be enacted into law. These recommendations, and subsequent actions by parliamentary bodies, are landmarks in the history of Anglo-Saxon sexual jurisprudence. At the time of this writing, none of the other 49 American states has changed its statutes to incorporate this recommendation of the American Law Institute.

Before making any further remarks, I want to state quite clearly and emphatically that I am in complete agreement with these recommendations. Sexual relations which occur between consenting adults in private places are simply no business of the law, and the present statutes which cover them should be removed from the books. But it is important to ask this question: what *effect* would this change in the law have on current relations between homosexuals and the courts? The evidence presented in this chapter makes it quite clear what effect this change would have. *It would have no effect.* We have already seen that while an arrest will occasionally be made, under these statutes, in a private place, by and large these laws are already a dead letter. The vast majority of homosexual acts never come to the attention of law enforcement agencies, and the vast majority of those which do come to the attention of these agencies do so because of activity which goes on in public places. One of the reasons an august legal body, such as the American Law Institute, can advocate such a change in the law is that the legal profession already knows that these laws are dead. It knows that they are not enforced to any significant extent, and that they cannot be enforced because of the search-and-seizure provisions of the Constitution. Nor would anybody want them enforced, because if they were fully enforced, literally millions of citizens would be arrested, including a very large number of married couples.

My point is simply this: it is quite desirable that these laws be removed from the books. They *are* unjust, and unjust statutes should be abolished even if they are not currently being enforced. The very existence on the statute books of unjust and unenforceable laws is discrediting to our entire legal system, as a number of writers have pointed out. But while this is a desirable aim, let it be made clear that such a change would have no significant effect on the life of the American male homosexual. The problems which he faces are, basically, not legal problems. They are *social* problems of a much more subtle kind, and in order for these problems to be solved, fundamental changes in the public attitude toward homosexuality will have to occur. If the proposed changes in the law are to represent a first step toward a significant change in public attitude, then they are intelligently conceived. If, on the other hand, they are to take place in the absence of any further changes on the part of the larger society in its attitude toward homosexuality, then they will accomplish nothing.

This view of homosexual law reform is not just a speculation. It has been corroborated by a series of interviews I have conducted with homosexuals who live or have lived in Chicago. Since Chicago has been, for well over five years, free from laws prohibiting homosexual relations between consenting adults in private, we must ask the question, has any significant change in the texture of homosexual life occurred in that city since the law was put into effect? The answer to this question is, clearly, no. On the basis of this special effort which I made to interview homosexuals in the city of Chicago and those who formerly lived there but have come out to the West Coast, I find that the general problems of the homosexual are exactly the same as they are in California. All the descriptive and theoretical statements contained in this book apply with the same degree of accuracy to Chicago as they do to San Francisco or Los Angeles. As a matter of fact, one can go further: homosexuals in Chicago have had somewhat *more* trouble with the law *since the enactment of the new penal code* than have homosexuals in San Francisco during the same period of time. One of the leading baths in Chicago and several of the more prominent gay bars were raided during that period and a number of respectable citizens were arrested during these raids. This has not happened in San Francisco during this same time period. Of course, one can say that these raids and arrests were not made under the provisions of the law that we are talking about. But this is precisely the point. The police do not generally use the sodomy laws against homosexual behavior in private as a means for arresting homosexuals in any state. They use provisions such as disorderly conduct, lewd and lascivious behavior, solicitation, etc., for purposes of arrest. When individuals *are* charged with violation of the sodomy laws (or oral copulation laws) it is because of behavior in public places. Licenses of bars and baths can be revoked by state administrative agencies on the grounds that a number of such arrests have occurred on the premises. The statutes prohibiting homosexual acts between consenting adults in private are simply not an issue in such legal encounters. Hence we do not expect that their abolition would have any effect on homosexual life and, as we have seen in Chicago, it has had no effect.

Let us be clear about what we are doing. Homosexual law reform must mean something more than merely the abolition of the sodomy laws, or it will mean nothing. It must go further than simply the elimination of an unenforced law from the statute books, or else it will go nowhere. Its ultimate aim must be to bring about substantial changes in the larger society—changes which will go much further than those legal alterations recommended by the American Law Institute. If it does not do this, a movement for homosexual law reform will be as moribund as the law which it seeks to abolish.

Solicitation and the Model Penal Code

A sad fact about the American Law Institute's Model Penal Code is that it contains a provision which reads as follows:

> Section 251.3. *Loitering to Solicit Deviate Sexual Relations.*
>
> A person is guilty of a petty misdemeanor if he loiters in or near any public place for the purpose of soliciting or being solicited to engage in deviate sexual relations.

It is not at all clear from reading the text of the Code whether or not "public place" includes bars. More importantly, this Section does not distinguish solicitation which would offend ordinary persons, who were in an ordinary "public place" in the usual course of their day, from harmless inquiry by one homosexual to another as to his interest in a mutual sexual experience.

Does it make any sense to "legalize" homosexual acts if it is still illegal for one man to invite another to participate in such a newly legalized act? One sometimes wonders to what extent the American Law Institute was really interested in changing the wrongness of the current attitude toward homosexuality or whether it was simply interested in getting an unenforced law off the books, in order to make the statutory provisions conform more to current police practice. If the latter was their aim, the Model Penal Code is written admirably. However, especially since we know that the sodomy laws are currently a dead letter, Section 251.3 perpetuates a very bad aspect of current policy, one that really counts heavily in the lives of very many homosexual men.

6

The Crime Against Nature

From the time of its Biblical prohibition (Leviticus 18:22 and 20:13), right down to the present day, homosexual behavior has been considered so horrible that the statutory prohibitions against it have merely alluded to it. For centuries it was referred to as "that abominable sin not fit to be named among Christians." The current statutes are generally not any clearer. In 13 states the term "sodomy" is used; one state labels the crime "buggery"; 19 states use the label "crime against nature"; and six use a combination of the latter with "sodomy." As we have seen previously, sexual relations between consenting adults in private are not very much the concern of law enforcement agencies, but instead their attention is directed to acts taking place in public places.

It is very instructive, however, to consider just what is meant by the term "crime against nature," for as has been pointed out by a number of legal scholars, this is one of the very few categories of crime in which the victim is not another person, but is rather "nature." This sounds very strange. Just what do we mean by "nature"? My point in this chapter shall be that nature has a very special meaning and that in order to understand what is meant by the term "crime against nature," we shall have to look backward to the origin of the concept of nature, which lies in early Greek thought.

Perhaps I owe the reader an explanation for a somewhat detailed excursion into the history of Greek philosophy, the origins of a difficult philosophical concept, and the study of its fate at the end of the Middle Ages. I have two reasons for discussing this material in the present context of our study of male homosexuality. In the first place, it is not really possible to understand the meaning of the legal statutes against homosexuality unless we understand what the term "nature" means in the phrase "crime against nature." As we shall see, it has a very particular meaning which does not mean nature in the ordinary sense of the term; it does not mean nature in the sense of the world of trees, flowers, animals, etc. In the second place, the problem of nature is by no means a dead issue, and it is particularly in a case like homosexuality that the issue is raised in contemporary contexts, for when homosexual behavior is discussed, many of those who are opposed to it describe it as "unnatural." Without understanding what is meant by the idea of nature and, therefore, of natural behavior, it is not really possible to understand the bases for the criticism of homosexuality as unnatural behavior. Consequently, I must beg the reader's indulgence for offering a discussion which draws material from the history of Greek and early modern philosophical thought, because it is of genuine importance for our study here.

What did the Greeks mean by the term "nature"? Aristotle, who devotes a section of his *Metaphysics* to a direct analysis of the meaning of the term, writes, "nature in the primary and strict sense is the essence of things which have in themselves, as such, a source of movement" (*Metaphysics*: 1015a, 13–15). It is, of course, impossible to understand what Aristotle means without explication, for although all the words which are used in this translation are words which are familiar to us from everyday use, they, like the term "nature" itself, have particular meanings here and cannot be understood without an explication of those meanings. By "things which have in themselves, as such, a source of movement," Aristotle refers to all living creatures, i.e., both plants and animals. On reflection, it is easy to see that living beings do have, within themselves, a source of movement, whereas non-living objects, such as stones and mountains, do not. (Water is a special case, since for Aristotle what the Greeks referred to as the simple bodies, namely, earth, air, fire, and water, were also things which had in themselves a source of movement, but we need not be further concerned with them here.) But in what sense can we imagine that plants have a source of movement within themselves? The answer to this question becomes clear when we understand what Aristotle meant by movement. When he uses the term he does not simply mean locomotion, although *animals* do, of course, have that property. He really means the tendency to grow and develop and, in this sense, it is easy to see that an acorn, for example, has a source of movement within itself, since, from its own insides, it is able to develop into an oak tree.

By "essence" Aristotle means that attribute (or attributes) which defines the being in question, which makes it what it truly is. The essence of a pen is to be written with; the essence of an acorn is to become an oak tree. When we speak of an acorn, since it is a living creature, we could also say that its *nature* is to become an oak. The nature of a living being is that source of its growth, organization, and behavior *within itself* which makes it what it is and makes it do what it does.

Why does an acorn become an oak? Because, for Aristotle, it is in the nature of acorns to become oaks. Unless impeded by some outside force, they will do so. Although rain, proper soil, etc., are necessary for such development, no outside force is the decisive cause of this change. It is because of forces *within* the acorn itself—its nature, primarily—that it normally grows to be the type of being it does.

Collingwood stated that for the Greeks, "the world of nature is saturated or permeated by mind" (Collingwood, 1960, p. 3). He speaks of the seed, and says, "The seed only grows *at all* because it is working at becoming a plant . . . because it *wants* to become a plant" (*ibid.*, p. 84). In the strict sense, this remark by Collingwood is an overstatement. We must not think that the Greeks quite thought that there was a little mind in every seed consciously planning the operations which would turn this seed into the plant. And yet Collingwood has given us a real insight into the Greek view of nature in his statement, for the classical conception did postulate a *soul* in all living beings, which soul desired to embody in the matter in which it was situated the full form of the species of which it was a member—its complete (mature) nature or essence.

The soul in the seed perceives the form of the mature plant and so moves or causes the seed to grow into this plant. The presence of a soul in all living creatures, as well as the simple bodies and the heavenly spheres, is what is meant by Plato's statement that "... all things are full of Gods" (*Laws*, 899b, 9). The similarity of this view to primitive forms of animism is quite obvious. For the Greek writers to which we have referred, the doctrine is much more subtle and refined, and therefore less starkly anthropomorphic. Nevertheless, it is clear that Collingwood has discerned the basic identity of the primitive and the classical philosophies of nature. This philosophy implies that living beings must strive toward their natural end, which is the goal prescribed by nature. This goal is the achievement of the true form of the being, the mature, complete adult form of the species of which it is a member. Connected with this view of being is the idea of *potentiality*, which means that the members of a species have the ability (unless thwarted by external or "accidental" forces) to realize their true nature. They have the potentiality to *actualize* the form of the mature member of the species, which form is apprehended by their soul. Rather than speak of soul, we could speak of an *active tendency* working within the being to realize this true nature. Thus, when Aristotle speaks of movement, he does not mean just locomotion, but basically refers to the actualization of that which is potential. Natural beings have active tendencies within them working toward this end, whereas if non-living things are to attain a certain form (for example, a piece of stone becoming a sculpture) there must be an outside force with the new form in *its* mind to affect this change (i.e., an artist).

The Law of Nature

The doctrine of "natural law" or "the law of nature" is the application of the conception of the universe implied in the classical idea of nature to the world of human experience.

Professor John Wild, an advocate of natural law theory, defines natural law as follows: "By natural law, or moral law, I mean a universal pattern of action applicable to all men everywhere, required by human nature itself for its completion" (Wild, 1953, p. 64).

The reader will see that a "human nature" which requires a universal pattern of action in order to complete itself is a "nature" which is conceived in accordance with the Aristotelian philosophy of nature which we have discussed above. What this philosophy says is that all men have certain inherent active tendencies toward a particular mode of life, which is the natural way to live. In order that they realize this kind of existence, they must act in accordance with certain rules. The equation by Wild of "moral law" with "natural law" indicates that natural law theory postulates a sufficient degree of freedom in man's nature so that he can choose the good (i.e., the natural) over the bad (i.e., the unnatural). When a man consistently chooses the natural or appropriate course of behavior, he will develop into a mature member of his species and therefore become most truly human.

It is important here to note the connection between the idea of natural law and the realm of law and politics. If there is such a thing as a universal pattern of action which men need to follow in order to realize their true nature, then the purpose of the state or the social order must be to encourage or enforce action which follows this pattern and discourage or prohibit action which violates it. To do this, many kinds of devices can, and have been, used. Basically the policy of "the carrot and the stick" is most generally felt to promote desired activity. This means, to reduce a complex matter to its most basic components, two kinds of political agents concerned with natural practice: policemen and moral leaders. The former punish moral deviations from the law of nature; the latter encourage proper, natural behavior. Thus we see clearly, as an example of "the stick," why deviant sexual practices are defined in many of our American statute books as "the crime against nature." When we say that deviant sexual practice is unnatural or against nature, we mean that it violates or goes against the inherent active tendency in all humans toward a particular kind of sexual activity.

In this connection, it must be remembered that the laws which prohibit homosexual practice are not written in such a way as to cover homosexual practice specifically or to cover homosexual practice alone. A state law prohibiting "the crime against nature" also prohibits a great amount of sexual activity that goes on between heterosexuals, including married couples. Whenever a married couple engages in anal intercourse, they are violating the state law which prohibits "the crime against nature" exactly as much as two men who might be engaging in the same kind of activity in an apartment down the street. In other words, the law prohibits certain kinds of *acts* and is not concerned with the sexual feelings of the individuals who engage in those acts.

The Fate of Nature

For Aristotle, the existence of nature was obvious or self-evident; he felt it would be absurd to attempt its demonstration (*Physics* 193a, 1–9). Yet in a passage a few pages further along in the *Physics*, Aristotle also says that it would be absurd to hold a teleological view of living things if we maintain at the same time a non-teleological conception of the heavenly bodies and their motion (196a, 25–196b, 5). By "teleological" we mean that goals or ends of processes are postulated as active agents in their own realization. For example, the goal of the acorn, i.e., an oak tree, was somehow present in the soul of the acorn and so it was acting all the time and directing the acorn in such a way that this goal could be realized in the actual world.

And yet it has come to pass that adherents of natural law are now forced into taking a teleological approach to certain aspects of man's experience, while at the same time maintaining a non-teleological approach, not only to the heavenly bodies and their motion, but to the whole of the physical and biological sciences and a good part of the social sciences and psychology as well. This paradoxical situation is a direct result of several factors, chief of which was the abandonment of nature as a category of explanation by the developing natural sciences. We often hear of the great scientific revolution of the sixteenth and seventeenth centuries. One could, with much justice, characterize this great intellectual change as the progressive abandonment of nature, in the sense in which we have defined the term here, in one field of scientific endeavor after the other.

It is not possible to identify one single event in the history of late medieval or early modern European thought and say, "*This* is where the change began." However, the intellectual ferment going on among certain scholastic writers in the fourteenth century may perhaps provide a convenient starting point to trace the central factors in the rise of modern science.

Whether they believed altogether in what they wrote, or whether they merely contrived an ingenious rhetorical device for the purpose of avoiding the label of heresy, a number of fourteenth-century philosophers took the following position: since God is omnipotent, He is capable of creating any sort of universe He desires; thus, current explanations of the universe are not the only possible theoretical system that can be imagined. If God chose, He might have created the universe along other lines.

This argument, which used theology against official philosophy, was a powerful agent in encouraging speculation about novel and unfashionable cosmologies. Because most late medieval theorists of science were much more given to philosophy than to experimental work, the practical fruits of this expansion of thought were not seen in the fourteenth century. But several thinkers appeared whose doctrines were so radical that even today they seem contemporary. Chief among these men was William of Ockham.

Ockham is known for several doctrines, almost all of which were either explicitly anti-Aristotelian or used against Aristotle's system. The so-called Ockham's Razor, or doctrine of economy in theory, while not new, was of great influence in the decline of the Aristotelian system of nature. Ockham's Razor tells us that in the formation of a theory, entities should not be multiplied without necessity. The simplest or most economical theory which can explain a particular subject matter is therefore the preferable one.

William of Ockham and his school did not destroy medieval science, a science which was based on the Aristotelian conception of nature, but they laid the conceptual groundwork for its destruction and provided a philosophical base for the work of later centuries. The actual demise of Aristotelian science could only come about by its replacement with an alternative system. This the Ockhamites and other fourteenth-century scholastics could not supply, since they did little, if any, actual experimentation.

The names of the great figures in the scientific revolution are well known: Copernicus, Brahe, Kepler, Galileo, Bacon, Descartes, Harvey, and Newton (to make a somewhat arbitrary list). Rather than go into a detailed description of how the concept of nature in all its diverse scientific forms was replaced by a new system of explanation, it will hopefully be sufficient for our purposes to give a general outline of the essential factors in this process of replacement.

On the most basic level there was a great spread of interest in actual empirical and experimental laboratory work. Tycho Brahe, for example, collected volumes of astronomical observation, which were later used by Kepler. The scientists of local mechanics, the most famous of whom was Galileo, conducted numerous experiments with falling bodies, inclined planes, projectiles, etc. The biologists, including Vesalius, and especially Harvey, dissected bodies and applied the comparative method to the study of human physiology.

The result of all this experimental work was a real beginning of an understanding of the rules or laws which govern the workings of the phenomena under observation. The emphasis shifted from Why? to How? What was now wanted were complete, detailed descriptions, based on careful observation, of the actual events which went on in the skies, in human bodies, and in physics laboratories. Thus, one of the decisive changes which distinguishes the modern era in science from earlier times is the shift in emphasis from speculation alone to the development of theory grounded in empirical study (see Crombie, 1959).

The idea of nature was not "disproved" but abandoned. Actually, it is not capable of refutation by empirical data, but the crucial point is this: when it became possible to describe and explain the phenomena of the sciences by detailed mathematical and mechanical explanations, nature was no longer found necessary or even helpful as a theoretical framework for scientific explanation. Empirical investigations brought the downfall of nature by providing new explanations, on the basis of which predictions could be made and the intricacies of phenomena described in great detail. When these were provided, nature appeared useless and was abandoned. For example, it was only possible to maintain that fire "rose upward" because it was its nature to move away from the center of the universe (for Aristotle, this was the center of the earth) as long as a good physical theory of fire was unavailable. When this was supplied, the Aristotelian explanation of fire collapsed.

Thus, nature started to decline with William of Ockham. By the time the science of Copernicus, Galileo, and Newton had become a reality, it was already gone from physical science. It was not until the time of Charles Darwin, however, that nature was ousted from biology, the realm in which it had originated, at least with Aristotle, and had found itself most at home. (It is probably not really appropriate here to discuss at any length the idea that Aristotle's categories fit best *biological* inquiry, but it might be pointed out that Aristotle was, in fact, the leading biologist of the ancient world and that it is probably no accident that his conception of nature is most happily applied to biological entities.)

Darwin's great contribution to the philosophy of science was not simply the notion of evolution or the concept that man and apes descended from a common ancestor. Although the "Copernican revolution" was said to have "insulted man's egoism" by making the sun, rather than the earth, the center of the universe, and the "Darwinian revolution" was said to have done the same by showing our primate friends to be relations, the ultimate philosophical import of these movements of thought was of a different, much more abstract, kind. Copernicus paved the way for a mechanical and mathematical explanation of astronomical phenomena and thus began the demolition of Aristotelian physical science. Darwin, whose great contribution was the detailed explanation of evolutionary change by means of the mechanism of natural selection, showed how it was possible to explain the *origin* of the diverse forms of life by a *non*-teleological approach, and thus his work made Aristotelian biological science obsolete. To quote John Dewey, "The Darwinian principle of natural selection cuts straight under this philosophy. If all organic adaptations are due simply to constant variation and the elimination of those variations which are harmful in the struggle for existence that is brought about by excessive reproduction, there is no call for a prior intelligent causal force to plan and preordain them" (Dewey, 1910).

With the development of modern genetics and the conception of mutations, the decline of the Aristotelian explanation of living species is complete. Further, modern biology, which appears to be drawing closer to the physical sciences through biochemistry and biophysics, has achieved a power of explanation such that teleological concepts are altogether forgotten. Purpose, end, goal, and other teleological notions no longer serve any useful purpose in biological science except when a human mind is thought to contain them. It is true that these concepts are sometimes used as a shorthand form when the non-teleological phraseology would be more cumbersome. However, the "purposive regulative principle," to use Dewey's term for nature, has altogether vanished from modern science and is no longer in use in any fundamental way. We no longer need to explain the development of an oak from an acorn by means of a soul in the acorn which conceives of the form of the mature oak and directs the seed to movement in this direction, when we can account for this change by means of a detailed physical-biological mechanism. To be sure, this change of explanation does not prove that no soul, nature, or essence is at work. It merely renders these conceptions superfluous.

Conclusion

I have taken the risk of losing the reader's attention by delving into a philosophical analysis of the concept of nature, for I felt it was very important to understand the meaning of the statutory term "crime against nature" and—probably more important—to understand the general conceptual framework which underlies the notion that certain kinds of sexual behavior, including a great deal that takes place between married couples, is contrary to the law of nature, or is unnatural. It might be remarked here that this discussion of the idea of nature would be just as appropriate in a book on contraception as in one on homosexuality, for it is the contention of opponents of contraception that the use of devices to prevent procreation violates natural law or is unnatural. Lying behind this contention, and the contention that anal intercourse between a married couple is unnatural, is exactly the same philosophy of nature that lies behind the prohibitions against homosexual behavior. The underlying notion is that the purpose of sexual behavior is procreation and that therefore the *only* acceptable form of sexual behavior is penis-in-vagina, and that anything outside of this, or anything which interferes in any way with the procreative aspect of sexuality, is contrary to nature. Such interference might come from the insertion of a diaphragm over the cervix of the female's uterus, or it might come from the wife bringing the husband to orgasm by fellatio, or it might come from the husband having intercourse with his wife anally—or, of course, it might come from the homosexual relations between those individuals whose lives we are examining in the present book.

The purpose of this chapter is to show that the idea of natural law, in the sense in which it is used by those who oppose homosexual behavior, contraception, and unorthodox sexual practices between married couples, is based on a philosophy of science which is no longer acceptable. It is certainly possible to criticize any of these activities on the grounds that they violate the moral law, as revealed by the deity through revelation. Since this is a scientific book and since, in order to deal with the religious arguments—numerous and complex—around this subject, we would need to make an extensive study of religious thought, involving both sexual and other matters, the present writer is going to take the very welcome opportunity of avoiding this area entirely and will deal with the problem of homosexuality from a purely secular point of view—praying that he can do an adequate job in this dimension.

7
○
● ●

The Development of
Sexual Identity

In this chapter and the one following, we will attempt to explain the origins of sexuality and of homosexual behavior. The present chapter will introduce some fundamental concepts of social psychology which will serve to help us understand the general development of sexual behavior. We will be especially concerned with the question of instinct versus learning as the basis for sexual identity and behavior.

The Problem of Action in the World

Man's central problem is to find meaningful action by which he can engage himself in the world. Since he is an energy-converting organism, he needs to act. Since he is a symbolic animal, he needs to render that action meaningful by relating it to the framework of symbols which he has learned from his culture. Unlike lower animals, man has a minimum of instinctual cues which could direct his behavior. The motives which govern his action are *learned in social interaction* with other people. This has several consequences. In the first place, it gives him a much wider range of possible kinds of action. By freeing him from the constraint of instinctual drives, the symbolic learning process permits man to develop diverse and often conflicting patterns of thought and behavior. It permits the development of complex modern civilizations with pluralistic subcultures.

At the same time as social learning permits a wide possibility for different kinds of action, it also leads to a problem of predictability in human life, for it is not always possible to tell what the next person is up to. Thus, there need to be socially structured ways of predicting the behavior of other human beings. Society provides, in part, a solution to this problem by setting up certain norms or rules to govern human conduct. These vary, of course, from society to society, and they also vary a great deal within any complex modern society. But there is no society without rules or norms. The problem for the *individual* is to learn to act in accord with the norms of his society or social group. The problem for *society* is to make consistent learning of these social rules possible, by making the rules clear and by developing a consistent set of rewards and punishments to induce the individual to conform his behavior to the rules. When large areas of behavior are unregulated by social controls, there exists a state of normlessness, or what the French sociologist, Emile Durkheim, called *anomie*. Anomie is a concept which refers to a particular state of affairs in society. It means that the rules which govern behavior are not clear and thus people don't know what to do. At a later point in this volume we will want to use Durkheim's concept in our discussion of the problem of homosexuality.

But the child does not learn to act correctly simply by reading from a rule book. He does not learn what is proper social behavior in the way in which an adult learns, for example, the rules which govern the filing of an income tax report. He learns them through interaction with the significant people in his environment, particularly his parents. And he learns these rules in intimate connection with the development of his own sense of self or his own identity. In other words, the rules are not learned in an intellectualized way, but they are incorporated into the very fiber of his being—his self-concept and sense of his own identity as a person. Social norms are literally *built into* the individual's mind. If the process is successful, he will not view these rules as something imposed upon him from without, but will see them as something which developed "naturally" from within his inner conscience. They become *his* rules and not just society's.

This process happens through the development of the sense of self. The philosopher George Herbert Mead raised the question as to how we learn to associate a certain body and its actions with a sense of "me" or of self. His answer was that you come to know who you are by taking the attitude toward yourself of someone who knew you and knew who you were long before you did, namely, your parents. The individual develops a sense of who he is by incorporating or internalizing the attitude toward himself which his parents have toward him. They hold attitudes toward him before he even develops a sense of his own identity, and it is through the child's incorporation of these attitudes that, in fact, his sense of identity is developed. In other words, as a child, one is told who one is. One is told what things are possible and what things are not possible, and this the child imbibes un-questioningly right along with his mother's milk. Conscious-ness is thus a social product. The sense of self, and the self-concept in all its ramifications, are dependent upon the definition of the individual which he gets from the significant people around him.

This process goes on, to a large extent, through the follow-ing mechanism: The parent defines certain kinds of action and behavior as definitely good or bad which cannot be questioned by the child. Thus, the child comes to accept uncritically certain perceptions of the world as a heritage from his parents. This is why children believe in the kinds of things that their parents teach them. This is what makes culture possible and what makes the transmission of social values and norms possible.

The psychoanalyst John Bowlby (1961) speaks of the "pri-mary anxiety" of the child. This primary anxiety is the fear that he will lose the parent, that the parent will go away or abandon him. The child learns to ward off this anxiety by un-consciously developing a certain kind of world view. The child's ego learns to view the world and to behave in accordance with the wishes of the parent. Thus, his perceptions of reality and his actions are structured in certain directions, in accord with the parental perceptions and views of acceptable be-havior. We might, if we like, say that the child's perceptions are constricted or skewed in a certain direction, but we should add that this is true for us all. We all "block out" certain aspects of reality, and the difference between cultures is largely a difference in the way that perceptions are skewed. We all skew our perceptions in order to avoid anxiety, and thus the differences in our views of reality and, consequently, in the possibilities for anxiety-free action are quite striking. Conceptions of reality vary greatly from culture to culture, but they also differ within the same large civilization, such as our own, for the differences in world view and thus of child-rearing practices from one apartment to the next in a large urban complex may be very striking indeed.

Self-Concept and Self-Esteem

"Self-esteem" means the individual's sense of his own worth. It is a part of the individual's concept of himself and it is a crucial indicator of his state of mental well-being. The child's self-esteem is dependent upon his parents' definition of his own value. When he does what his parents want him to do, he is defined as good, and so he feels good; when he does what he is not supposed to do, his parents define him as bad, and then he *defines himself* as bad, and his self-esteem drops. When Freud spoke of the internalization of culture in the superego, he was referring to the process by which the conscience is built into the child through its interactions with the parents. The child adopts the parents' values in order to avoid the anxiety caused by the implied threat of loss of the parents' love if he does something they think is bad. In effect, the child says, "You no longer have to punish me, father. I will punish myself now; I have done something bad." In other words, the child's self-esteem falls when he experiences feelings, or engages in actions, which have been defined by the parents as bad, and which, in this process of socialization, he has come to define for *himself* as wicked. In essence, this is what socialization is all about. Its full development leads to the orientation of the child toward the general society and makes it possible for him to become a member of the larger society rather than only of his individual family. His self-esteem becomes dependent on both his internalized values and the reflected appraisals from others about him.

It should not be inferred from this discussion that the development of the self stops at age five—or at any age, for that matter. The school-age years are crucial to the development of the child's sense of self-value. His interactions with his peers throughout childhood and adolescence play a vital role in the formation of his sense of identity—including his sexual identity. As a matter of fact, one of the flaws in much current psychiatric writing about human sexuality is the idea that it is only the parent-child interactions which are significant in the development of sexual feelings. While these *are* a crucial factor, a full explanation of any given adult's sexual patterns must take into account the vital years between the beginning of schooling and the end of adolescence. It is during these years that the individual learns a great deal about who he is, what he can and cannot do, and how his age-mates will respond to his actions. This learning is crucial for the development of identity in general, and sexual identity in particular. It was certainly justified for Freud to place such great emphasis on the first five years of life, for these years had been so neglected and misunderstood prior to psychoanalysis. But perhaps the pendulum has swung too far: we have been operating as if it is only these years that are of significance in the development of human sexual behavior. Such is not the case.

Vicissitudes of Self-Concept: Deviance and Mental Illness

It is now easy to see that we *all* have an idiosyncratic resolution of the socialization process. We all get somewhat different messages from our parents; we all incorporate slightly different values into our self-concept, and our self-esteem is affected differentially by different kinds of perceptions and actions. The life task of each individual is to maintain a sense of his own self-value as he participates in action in the world.

Deviant behavior is simply a type of self-esteem maintenance which leads to behavior not accepted by the general culture. For example, in drug addiction the individual maintains his self-esteem by chemical methods which are not accepted by the culture at large. He derives his self-esteem from taking a drug into his system (Hoffman, 1964). In some cultures this is more acceptable than in others, and in all cultures there are certain drugs which are more acceptable than other drugs. In our culture, for example, heroin use is defined as deviant because the culture does not accept this method of self-esteem maintenance. On the other hand, our culture readily accepts and encourages forms of self-esteem maintenance which other cultures frown upon, e.g., the maintenance of one's sense of self-value by the accumulation of material goods.

The label "deviant behavior" does not imply that the individual who engages in deviance necessarily suffers because of it. Deviance implies only that the individual engages in behavior which society condemns. If his own superego or conscience approves of this behavior, he may have no internal conflict about it. The results of a deviant act may, of course, lead an individual into some kind of overt conflict with society—a continuum which ranges from merely being viewed as eccentric all the way to execution. I don't mean to say that many deviants do not have a great deal of inner conflict regarding their deviant actions. Very many of them do. I only want to indicate that deviance does not necessarily produce a sense of guilt, i.e., some internalized prohibition concerning the deviant action.

Mental illness, on the other hand, is properly conceptualized somewhat differently than deviance. This term is applied to the individual whose early training, especially in the family, does not prepare him for a role in which he can create enough of a sense of self-esteem and of meaningful action in adult life (Becker, 1964). The mentally ill cannot ward off anxiety because they literally cannot conceptualize action outside a restricted range—a range of possible action which is too limited for the society in which they find themselves. The mentally ill person is brought up in a family which is not wholly suited to produce members of the society to which it belongs. By definition, such an individual suffers psychologically from his behavioral ineptitude in adult life. The deviant may or may not be mentally ill. The mentally ill person may or may not be deviant in behavior. Deviance is a sociological term and mental illness is a psychological one. Deviance is a label attached to individuals because they violate social norms. Mental illness is a diagnosis made on the basis of certain types of reported unhappiness on the part of individuals.

The Question of Sexual Drives

Freud promulgated the idea of an inherited constitutional bisexuality in humans. This refers to the notion that individuals have an inherited tendency to choose both heterosexual and homosexual love objects. We are probably all familiar with what Freud called the Oedipus complex. Around ages three to five, the young boy develops a sexual desire for his mother, which ultimately has to be repressed but which forms the basis for heterosexual feelings in later years. It is not so well known that Freud also spoke of a "negative Oedipus complex," which refers to the boy's love for the father.

According to Freud, this complex is also normally present in the developing life of the child.

The notion that at certain points of their lives individuals spontaneously develop sexual feelings for particular persons is a doctrine of inherited ideas. The whole notion of an inherited bisexuality has been criticized by Sandor Rado (1940), who points out that neither biological nor psychological evidence will support such a theory. What Rado wishes to do, however, is to strike out the idea of inherited homosexuality from the concept of bisexuality and leave us with a constitutional drive toward heterosexuality. In this he is followed by a group of psychoanalysts (of whom the best known perhaps is Irving Bieber) who have rewritten the Freudian theory of homosexuality in order to remove from it the idea of constitutionally inherited homosexuality (Bieber, 1962).

While I am in agreement with Rado and Bieber that the conception of an inherited bisexuality is both unnecessary and unsupportable, it seems to me that the criticism applies just as much to their notion of inherited heterosexual drives as to that Freudian theory which they are criticizing. In their writings, they offer no evidence for the existence of an inherited drive toward heterosexuality. One presumes, from a reading of their works, that their main evidence for this supposed drive is that the majority of persons they know are predominantly heterosexual. This seems to me a perfect example of what the philosopher of science, Ernest Nagel, calls a pseudo-explanation (1961, pp. 36–37). Nagel defines a pseudo-explanation as one "in which the premises simply rebaptize the facts to be explained by coining new names for them. The classical example of such pseudo-explanations is the butt of Molière's satire in which he ridicules those who explain the fact that opium induces sleep by invoking the dictum that opium possesses a dormative virtue. A less obvious illustration, sometimes found in popular expositions of science, is the explanation of the law that the velocity of a body remains constant unless the body is acted on by an unbalanced external force, because all bodies possess an inherent force of inertia. This is a pseudo-explanation, since the word 'inertia' is just another label for the fact stated in the law."

To explain the fact that most individuals in our culture are heterosexual by postulating an inborn drive toward heterosexuality really explains no more than when it was said that opium induces sleep because it possesses a dormative virtue. At least Freud's concept of bisexuality had something new about it (although it had plenty of historical antecedents). The Rado-Bieber revisionism is nothing more than a commonsense theory of the origins of sexual behavior, which turns out upon analysis to be not much of a theory at all. It represents, in my view, an attempt to tame Freud, or render him more "acceptable," by cutting out the unpalatable notion that all individuals have homosexual feelings.

Origins of Sexual Behavior

Where do sexual feelings originate? If neither homosexual nor heterosexual ideas pop into the head at certain developmental stages, then how can we explain the existence of such feelings in adults and many children? We must be frank to admit that the answer to this question is not as clear as we would like. However, the best available evidence indicates that the individual *learns* sexual responses in social interaction with his parents and peers. This learning is possible because of what I would call an *undifferentiated sexual potential* in the child. This might be thought of as an unformed drive which is not attached to any particular love object, but which develops a "content" by very complicated learning processes. As Frank Beach (1965) has pointed out, studies of mammals show that as one ascends the mammalian scale, there is a lessening hormonal control of sexual behavior and an increased control by the cerebral cortex. This means that the higher one goes in the primate scale, the more the sexual development of the organism is under the sway of learning, rather than of inherited factors.

In a fascinating series of studies of individuals with biological sexual abnormalities (pseudo-hermaphrodites), John Money, Joan G. Hampson, and John L. Hampson (1955) have accumulated a good deal of evidence that both gender identity (one's feelings of masculinity or femininity) and sexual object-choice (one's preference for a type of sexual partner) are due to social learning. Their evidence indicates that, at least insofar as these two factors are concerned, humans are *psychosexually neutral* at birth. The development of both gender identity and sexual object-choice is due to the extremely subtle interaction which goes on between the child and the significant persons in his environment. It is based on cues and signals which the parents transmit to the child as to his proper gender role and as to the kinds of sexual feelings which are permitted. As we saw in the previous pages, an individual's self-concept (and thus his conception of himself as masculine or feminine and his conception of what is sexually possible or impossible) is due to the messages he gets from his parents regarding what is permissible and impermissible behavior. The individual's sexual self-concept as well as the range of permissible sexual feelings are assimilated unconsciously.

As Harry F. Harlow has shown (1962), preventing certain kinds of parent-child interaction in lower primates leads to very peculiar adult sexual behavior. When male and female monkeys are reared in the presence of cloth mothers rather than real mothers, they are unable to develop appropriate adult sexual behavior. These monkeys, who were also denied any contact with other monkey infants, are not able to achieve sexual insertion and complete the full pattern of coitus. This is not due to a motor defect but to a lack of knowledge of what to do. These deficiencies are *not* corrected by repeated trial and error learning, although the same animals exhibit entirely normal performance in the traditional test for learning ability. Beach quotes Rosenblatt as follows: "As a social bond, sexual behavior grows out of affective reactions between the animals and is rooted in a general background of social responses developed earlier in life." Beach goes on to say, "observation of captive monkeys in the highly artificial laboratory environment suggests that the ontogeny of sexual activities is inextricably interwoven with the development of other forms of interpersonal behavior . . ." (Beach, 1965, p. 549). Since we know that as we ascend the mammalian scale, learning factors become more important the higher we go, we can postulate that if these factors are true for monkeys, it would seem they are true for humans. Thus, we conclude that learning factors play the predominant role in the development of sexual behavior. As John L. Hampson has written: "We conclude that an individual's gender role and orientation as boy or girl, man or woman, does not have an innate, preformed instinctive basis as some theorists have maintained. Instead the evidence supports the view that psychologic sex is undifferentiated at birth—a sexual neutrality one might say—and that the individual becomes psychologically differentiated as masculine or feminine in the course of the many experiences of growing up" (1965, p. 119). Hampson goes on to say, "As an alternative to employing a drive concept, it might be preferable to say simply that the erotically sensitive parts of the human body can be stimulated and used by oneself or another person, and that during the process of psychologic maturation and development erotic sensations become firmly associated with, and inextricably a part of, adult gender role" (*ibid.*).

Primary Genital Phobia

The American psychiatrist Harry Stack Sullivan coined the term "primary genital phobia" for a clinical phenomenon which we can explain in accord with the theoretical framework presented in this chapter. Sullivan talks about what he calls the "not-me." He defines this as "the organization of experience with significant people that has been subjected to such intense anxiety, and anxiety so suddenly precipitated, that it was impossible for the then relatively rudimentary person to make any sense of, to develop any true grasp on, the particular circumstances which dictated the experience of this intense anxiety" (Sullivan, 1953, p. 314). What Sullivan means is that the individual has feelings of a certain kind or attempts to engage in a particular form of behavior, and the reaction from the significant person or persons in the immediate environment *is so negative* that he immediately represses his feelings or his wish to act in a certain way. The feeling or wish is defined so negatively by the other person that it cannot be admitted as a part of one's own self. It is relegated to that part of the unconscious which Sullivan calls the "not-me." By this he means that it is not available for reflection or for correction in the light of new experience. It persists in the unconscious as a stumbling block to a more intelligent form of action. Sullivan goes on to say:

As I have said, very intense anxiety precipitated by a sudden, intense, negative emotional reaction on the part of the significant environment has more than a little in common with a blow on the head. It tends to erase any possibility of elaborating the exact circumstances of its occurrence, and about the most a person can remember in retrospect is a somewhat fenestrated account of the event in the immediate neighborhood. If, for example, a parent had a subpsychotic fear of the infant's becoming a lustful monster and has gone off the deep end whenever the infant was discovered to be holding the penis or fondling the vulva—then we expect that the personality of the infant as it develops will show a sort of hole in that area, in the sense that any approach to the genitals will ultimately lead to the appearance of a feeling which has scarcely evolved beyond sudden, intense, all-encompassing anxiety. (Pp. 314–15.)

The point to be made here is that a clinical phenomenon like primary genital phobia is an example of the way in which parental behavior determines sexual feelings by means of the effect of the parents' reactions to the child's unwitting behavior. These parental reactions affect the child through the child's self-conception and his self-esteem. The self-conception will be molded by the significant environment, and thus the gender identity and sexual identity of the child will become a product of his significant personal encounters.

The Question of Imprinting

In their work, Money and the Hampsons have hypothesized that gender identity and sexual object-choice are fixed during a period which coincides with the development of language, i.e., from 18–24 months of age. Their clinical experience indicates that a change in the sex in rearing of a child can be successfully imposed prior to this age, but that after two years there is a severe psychologic risk in an attempt at changing a child's gender identity. Hence, these authors postulate the importance of critical periods in the establishment of certain facets of gender role and they hypothesize that perhaps a learning process akin to the phenomenon of imprinting, seen in lower animals, could be involved. However, as Frank Beach remarked (1965, p. 128): "To date there is no reliable evidence that imprinting occurs in mammals."

Freudians have also insisted upon the critical importance of the first five years in the development of all the important facets of the personality, including sexual identity. While there is no question of the crucial importance of these years, the importance of later years has been especially underemphasized in the literature on sexual object-choice and the development of homosexuality. Here we have to distinguish between a number of various concepts, such as gender identity and sexual object-choice. It may well be true that what Stoller (1965) calls "core gender identity," the basic sense that one is a male or a female organism, *is* established during very early years. It is *not* true that sexual object-choice is always *fixed* during those same early years. As a matter of fact, clinical evidence overwhelmingly shows that there are many individuals who have a great degree of fluidity in their sexual object-choice well into adult life. Changes in sexual object-choice occur at all ages and in individuals in whom the issue of sexual object-choice was hitherto supposed to have been settled. For example, there are men who do not "come out" until they have already had years of heterosexual experience, been married, and fathered children. Then, for reasons which are so often unclear, they suddenly find themselves developing conscious homosexual desires during their 40's or 50's. A "reverse" phenomenon can occur. Gay men can decide that they are getting too old to make out well in, e.g., the bar scene, in which they have been involved for years. They may then establish an emotional relationship with a woman and can then find themselves developing a heterosexual erotic interest which they had never thought possible. People are really more diverse and their sexual orientations more complicated and changing than either the popular mind or many writers on human sexuality would have us believe.

8

○
• •

The Roots of
Homosexuality

In the last chapter we saw that the evidence presently available to students of human sexuality points strongly to the conclusion that sexual object-choice is basically a learned phenomenon. It is therefore related to many factors which act upon the individual's development during all phases of his life. With such a complexity of interacting relationships, it would, of course, be impossible to identify a single cause for homosexual preference. Nonetheless, I think we can point out *some* of the possible meanings which homosexual behavior has for different persons. One of the clear points of agreement among disparate schools in modern psychiatry and social science is—to put the matter in its simplest form—that the same things have different meanings for different people. For example, if a patient in analysis tells a dream about being driven through a countryside in a red car and then being taken to an old gothic house for a dinner party which includes his grandmother, his child, and an old sweetheart, we cannot immediately know what this dream means. Patients often imagine that the analyst can simply read the dream as if he had a secret code which will tell him immediately what a red car means, what a dinner party means, and so on. On the contrary, the only one who can "tell us" what this dream means is the patient himself, who can elaborate on his associations to the various elements of the dream. He would find that a red car, for instance, has a particular meaning in his life, and that the gothic house reminded him of some especially significant past event, and so forth. Thus, the meanings of the same dream elements for one person are usually quite different than for another.

The same rule of the variability of meanings holds for sexual preference. Two different men may engage in the same kind of sexual act, but this does not indicate that this behavior has the same meaning for both of them. Fellatio, for example, performed under the very same circumstances, e.g., in the baths, may have wholly different meanings for two different 30-year-old men who are performing it. In order to find out what this behavior does mean we would have to investigate the particular life history of the individual, ascertain his fantasies during the sexual act, and find out the present life circumstance that led him to the baths on this particular night.

What can we say, then, about homosexual behavior in general? Can we say anything at all about it? In spite of the caution I have proposed here, I think it is quite possible to say a good deal that is significant about the roots of homosexual behavior, for we find that when we do investigate individual lives, there are certain patterns which recur, and some of these we shall describe in the present chapter.

But we must insert yet another caution, one that is not sufficiently stressed when the psychodynamics of homosexual behavior are discussed in the literature. This is that it is much easier to explain pathological manifestations of a particular category of behavior than normal manifestations, and the more pathological the cases become, the easier they are to explain. If sexual behavior is learned, then all sexual object-choices can be explained in psychological and[or sociological terms. This would include normal heterosexual behavior as well as the most bizarre perversions. While, in this present chapter, I do not want to get into the controversy about whether or not homosexuality is an illness—a discussion of this controversy is reserved for the following chapter—I do at least want to emphasize that because those types of homosexual object-choice which are connected with some kind of trauma or unhappiness in childhood are the easiest to explain, the following pages may give the erroneous impression that all homosexual behavior can be explained in "symbolic" terms. Let me try to clarify this.

"Normal" Sexual Behavior

How can we explain heterosexual behavior if this too is a learned phenomenon? And if there is homosexual behavior which can be called non-pathological, can it be explained along the same lines? The answer to these questions becomes much more obvious when we reflect upon the reason why heterosexual behavior is the most common form of sexual behavior in our present society. The reason, I think, is very clear. It is because heterosexuality is encouraged and because homosexual behavior is discouraged. Consequently, it is the "natural" thing for young men to prefer girls as sexual objects. One need only reflect upon the content of the popular media to realize that the cues are all around us and that they exist in the most subtle as well as the most gross forms. Men learn heterosexual object-choice because no other object-choice is considered possible for them; that is, they are not allowed to conceive of the possibility that there can be another kind of sexual object other than the opposite sex. This starts at the earliest age when, for example, they play "house," a game in which roles are segregated according to sex; it continues throughout the development of the child and adolescent. The boy is given innumerable messages, both overt and covert, by his parents, his peers, and the culture at large, that relationships with girls are considered very desirable. But not only is he told that he should have relationships with girls, he is also *not given the alternative possibility*, that homosexual relationships are possible. This possibility is withheld from him by a combination of omission and prohibition. In other words, he is not taught that such things are possible, and so *he does not even conceive of it.*

If a conception of homosexual sex does, however, somehow manage to find its way into his consciousness, it is quickly obliterated by severe sanctions. The culture tells him that if he prefers men as sexual objects, he is not himself a real man; there is something wrong with him; he is queer. This message is given to him in such a way that it evokes uncanny feelings, what Sullivan describes as the "not-me." In other words, to use the vocabulary introduced in the last chapter, the male child is trained so that his self-esteem will suffer a severe drop if he conceptualizes intimate relations with another male. His self-concept is not permitted to entertain the notion of himself as a paramour of another male. This is forbidden. Any such notions are subject to immediate repression. If the thought of homosexual relations should happen to arise in his mind, about all the normal male has is a sort of uncanny feeling that these things are not part of his world. Although it is possible that he is not threatened by the thought of other men engaging in homosexual relations, even this tolerance has its limits. Non-homosexual men who come into contact with homosexual males who are together *as homosexuals*, e.g., at a gay dance club, often find that their lack of rational objection to homosexual behavior and their liberal tolerance for other styles of life simply do not go deep enough to prevent them from feeling acutely uncomfortable in the presence of men who are dancing together or embracing. I think we know enough about different mental states from psychoanalytic investigation to be fairly certain that this distaste—which the experiencing individual often himself believes to be "irrational"—is a product of his own unconscious identification with the other persons, specifically the homosexual males who are dancing together, and the consequent repression this empathic feeling needs to undergo as it meets the adverse definition of homosexual feelings present within the individual's conception of himself.

There are, of course, some men who are less subject to this kind of self-condemnation of homosexual feelings than are others. There is almost an infinite variation among families in the degree to which homosexual and heterosexual feelings are permitted or encouraged. In some families, as a number of psychoanalysts have pointed out, *heterosexual* feelings are explicitly discouraged as being wicked, while nothing is said about homosexual impulses, so that the child gets the message, even if covertly, that homosexual behavior may be less undesirable than heterosexual behavior.

We will not, of course, have a really satisfactory understanding of homosexuality until we understand what psychophysiological mechanisms are involved in the development of sexual excitation. We know why a man may be attracted to a certain kind of woman, but we don't actually know why he gets an erection when he is with her. In order to know this, we would have to know the relationship between the psychological factors involved in his attraction and the physiological mechanisms involved in the sexual response itself. About all we can say at this point in our knowledge of human sexuality is that sexual feelings seem to have their origin in the interpersonal relations that go on between the child and other people in his world, particularly his parents, but also other adults, his siblings, and his peers. We know that factors which affect the relations between individuals in the child's interpersonal world will also have profound effects on later sexual development. Evidence from animal studies, such as Harlow's, and from studies of other cultures, strongly supports this belief.

For a case in point, let me quote from Frank Beach's account of Davenport's report of gender-role training in a primitive society:

> From very early childhood boys and girls are physically segregated, trained in distinctly separate social roles, and prevented insofar as possible from learning anything about the opposite sex including even the details of physical appearance. Adult males and females intermingle only on special occasions and even then the forms of social exchange are highly constrained and narrowly limited. The combination of these factors has powerful effects on all forms of heterosexual interaction not

excluding marital relationships. Young men and women find the first stage of marriage to be, "one of the most excruciating periods of their entire life." The initial problem is not to achieve mutually satisfying genital union, but to overcome the shame and embarrassment of merely speaking to one another, even in privacy. A bride and groom often actively avoid each other whenever possible, and one or two years may elapse before they are sufficiently at ease to take joint residence in the dwelling which the husband has constructed. (Beach, 1965, p. 551.)

If it is true that adult sexuality is an outgrowth of early interpersonal relations, as studies of both other species and other societies, as well as our own, seem clearly to indicate, then what I have called the undifferentiated sexual potential may be directed in a number of different ways depending upon the interactions which occurred during childhood and youth. For most children, the close feelings they had toward their mother and father are prohibited from taking sexual form by the incest taboo, a taboo which is practically universal and which is probably necessary for the maintenance of society because it, in effect, socializes the child *out* of the family into the larger group (Parsons, 1954). The homosexual feelings which might develop toward the father or, after the father is prohibited as a sexual object by the incest taboo, toward other males, are—in our culture—removed by the general stricture which society places on homosexual desires. Thus, the child is left with heterosexual feelings directed toward those women who are outside his own immediate family. This is the "normal" pattern of sexual object-choice in our own society. However, in a complex pluralistic society such as our own, social norms are not learned uniformly, and the individual's family may, for one reason or another, not socialize him as the culture would desire. Thus, the heterosexual feelings which persist into adulthood may be accompanied by homosexual feelings which have arisen in the same way, i.e., in relation to the parents. Even with the fact of the incest taboo, homosexual feelings may still be present in conscious form and may be directed to other boys in the child's environment. In some cases, as has been indicated, the family may find these less "wicked" than the boy's heterosexual feelings and may unwittingly encourage the homosexual component by suppressing the other.

What I am trying to present here is an explanation of how homosexual feelings may arise in the child, in the absence of the very definite symbolic meanings which one would think they universally carry if one reads psychoanalytic writings on the matter. It is, of course, simpler to describe the "symbolic" forms of homosexual behavior, as we are now going to do, but it should not be thought that all homosexual behavior arises from such sources. One only has to reflect that normal *hetero*sexual behavior has itself to be accounted for as a product of learning in social interaction during the early years, and then one sees that not all sexual behavior can be explained in terms of very obvious "symbolic" patterns.

Earlier in the book, I promised to give an explanation for the fact that so many homosexual men do not develop an awareness of their homosexuality until they are many years past puberty. For example, I interviewed a physiologist who, looking back, realizes that he has always been gay, has never had any sexual interest in women, and has had sporadic overt homosexual contacts since childhood. Nevertheless, he did not realize he was homosexual until he was 27 and did not come out, in the sense of defining himself as such and entering the gay world, until after his 28th birthday. (He regrets this delay very much, as these were quite lonely years for him, and although he does not entirely escape loneliness now —since, like so many others, he too is searching for a stable relationship with another man—he feels he is much better off than when he was in his early 20's and did not know he was gay, yet had no heterosexual interests.)

I think this phenomenon can only be explained as being due to a combination of the two factors we have been discussing, namely, the failure of society to make people aware of homosexuality as an existent way of life (and of the existence of the gay world), and the strong repressive forces that prevent people from knowing what their real sexual feelings are. One might consider this phenomenon a psychological conspiracy of silence, which society insists upon imposing because of its belief that it thereby safeguards existent sexual norms.

A Case of Homosexuality

Let me now describe a patient whom I saw in clinical practice some years ago, one whom I have previously described in a somewhat different context (Hoffman, 1964). This individual was a young man in his 20's who came to see me about some neurotic problems, including sexual ones. He was an extremely promiscuous homosexual, who had had literally hundreds of sexual encounters. The figure 1,003 given for Don Giovanni might well have been surpassed by this individual in his constant search for sexual partners. One day, early in the treatment, on his way to my office, he saw what he regarded as an especially attractive young man. When he got into the office he made the statement that there must be something wrong with him, since he wanted to perform fellatio on every adolescent he saw.

His feeling was that his behavior was "sick," as he put it. At first I thought this was simply a feeling of guilt, and there is no question that he did have a great deal of guilt over his sexual activities. Later in the therapy, however, it became clear that something else was causing this feeling. When he saw a young man he found attractive, he did feel distressed, but he covered up this feeling right away by overlaying it with a feeling of sexual desire and then planning the conquest. The distressing feeling, which was his very first reaction to the person, and which actually got him interested in the young man in the first place, underwent a very quick repression.

What was this feeling about? My patient's reaction to an attractive male adolescent was one of acute bewilderment in the face of a painful situation. He saw the individual, and the individual's presence disturbed, confused, annoyed him in some inexplicable fashion. The young man's presence somehow made a call to action necessary in order to gain some form of mastery over the situation. What appeared superficially as merely a desire for a great deal of sexual pleasure was in reality a need to master a predicament which followed upon any chance encounter with a certain kind of individual.

This patient had suffered through a very trying childhood, in which his older brother had received all the attention and glory he felt he needed for himself. The result was that the patient developed a very low sense of self-value in relation to his brother. Somehow this crystallized in adolescence, when his brother's superiority seemed to overwhelm him. In reacting to the young men whom he desired sexually, he was transferring feelings from an earlier period of his life into the current situation. He was reacting to these young men as if they were his brother, and he was therefore faced with the same bewilderment, confusion, and sense of extremely low self-esteem in relation to them that he had earlier experienced in relation to the brother. The feeling was so acute that he needed to repress it immediately. His ego had found that a sexualized response was a way of solving the dilemma and so the promiscuous homosexual pattern was begun.

It is important to ask the crucial question: why was this unconscious problem sexualized? The answer is that by sexualizing the problem, our patient transformed a distressing situation into a pleasurable one. He had found no other way to deal with his feelings of envy, hostility, depression, all stemming from his sense of low self-value, which were developed in relation to his brother. Whenever he saw a young man who brought these feelings close to the surface he found himself in a psychological quandary. By transforming this distressing creature (the young man) into a creature from whom pleasure could be derived, he was able to transform the minus situation into a plus.

Our patient's sexual promiscuity was probably related to at least four factors. First, his hostility to the sexual partner could only stand repression through one sexual encounter. This meant that after the act was over, he wanted to get away from his partner as soon as possible. Second, he felt very guilty about his homosexuality and this also led to the desire to forget the individual with whom he had just had sex. Third, almost every new adolescent was a challenge to him: could he eliminate this particular individual as a constant reminder of his distress by permanently grouping him with the givers of pleasure—the young men who had made it possible for him to convince himself that his ego was able to handle the unconscious distress? Therefore, of course, virtually every young man he encountered became a candidate for seduction. Fourth, as was to be expected with such an unhappy background, his skill in interpersonal relationships was poor. A close, long-lasting relationship with another man was too much for him. He simply was not able to conceptualize such a complex interpersonal role. This was, of course, intimately tied up with his low self-esteem.

We see in this case the use of homosexual behavior as a way of handling a severe, problematic situation in one's life. It is a "reparative" device which the individual uses to solve particular life problems. Psychoanalytic literature contains many examples of homosexual behavior as a symbolic means for solving particular existential problems It would be well worth our time if we considered a few of the other meanings which certain kinds of homosexual behavior might have for some individuals.

Fellatio

Some homosexuals engage in behavior which is so irrational that it virtually requires a psychodynamic explanation. A good example of this is the case of the compulsive fellator who finds himself actually driven to engage in fellatio under what are sometimes situations of radical danger. This person frequently picks up rough-looking young men, e.g., hitchhikers and servicemen, and tries to persuade them to let him bring them to orgasm by fellatio. He is often a typical client of hustlers. As a result of his efforts, this individual frequently is assaulted and is occasionally murdered, although very often it is not clear from reading the press reports that there was a sexual basis to the crime.

What is the reason for this compulsive desire for fellatio? It seems that this particular manifestation of fellatio is very much like what the Biblical historian W. Robertson Smith referred to as a sacramental feast, in which the participant eats the flesh and drinks the blood of the divine animal during a primitive religious ceremony, in order to get the *mana* or vital power which is present within the animal. As Gilbert Murray noted, "the classical instance is the sacramental eating of a camel by an Arab tribe, recorded in the works of St. Nilus. The camel was devoured on a particular day at the rising of the morning star. He was cut to pieces alive, and every fragment of him had to be consumed before the sun rose. If the life had once gone out of the flesh and blood the sacrifice would have been spoilt; it was the spirit, the vitality, of the camel that the tribesmen wanted" (Murray, 1951).

The compulsive fellator is unwittingly re-enacting an ancient religious rite. By sucking the penis of what he believes to be an especially masculine male, he feels he is incorporating some of this masculinity and vitality into his own person. Obviously his sense of his own masculinity must be at a chronically low ebb in order for him to engage in this kind of magical behavior. This would account for the inexplicable nature of his search for sexual partners. He himself feels bewildered by the phenomenon and cannot explain why, during certain times, he feels an acute restlessness and needs to go out cruising in the car, looking for hitchhikers, sailors, or hustlers. In many cases where such individuals have been analyzed, it is found that this acute sense of sexual longing is preceded by some kind of blow to the self-esteem, so that the individual's sense of his own value has been pushed to a new low. His search for a sexual partner is therefore a search for a replenishment of his own vitality, and it is uncannily like the primitive search for the sacred animal whom he must consume in order to engage in a renewal of his own powers. For reasons which vary from case to case, such homosexual males have fixed upon the penis as being an especially powerful object and believe, at an unconscious level, that by taking the penis into their mouth, they can incorporate some of this power into themselves.

This explanation fits in very well with the well-known emphasis on penis size among male homosexuals. Any student of gay life can attest to the fact that very many male homosexuals are particularly fetishized on the size of the penis, and that this forms a recurrent topic of discussion among them. While this can partly be attributed to reasons no more pathological than the heterosexual male's interest in his partner's breast size, such an interest on the part of the homosexual male very often results in his going to great lengths to secure a partner with the largest possible penis. Often, this results in his taking risks which would be unnecessary if he were merely searching for a male sexual partner. A good deal of this behavior is so dangerous that it demands a psychoanalytic explanation, and the viewing of fellatio as a sacramental feast provides this kind of understanding of an otherwise inexplicable phenomenon.

Perhaps the reader may wonder why a "masculine" male would want to be the divine animal in a sacramental feast, i.e., be fellated (or take the insertor role in anal intercourse —for the receptor may prefer to incorporate the penis in this way). Obviously, many reasons would be involved. The individual may get a feeling of power from assuming what he feels is a "dominant" role with another male. Or he may be sexually excited by another man and wish to consummate that excitement by being physically stimulated to the point of orgasm. (These two possible explanations are not, of course, mutually exclusive.)

Since the receptor in a homosexual encounter may not achieve ejaculation, it is somewhat easier to explain insertion than its converse when considering homosexual sexual relations. Men, generally, like to have their penises stimulated. But it must again be emphasized that homosexuals often have sexual preferences for multiple acts. The fellator may get an erection because he is sexually aroused by sucking his partner's penis. He may then wish his partner to reciprocate the fellation, or, alternately, may masturbate himself to orgasm. Sometimes receptors do not achieve orgasm, e.g., during anal intercourse. But they may, after their partner's orgasm, then achieve ejaculation themselves—and the ways in which they might do this include all those which are physically possible.

Castration Anxiety

A classic psychoanalytic explanation used to account for the existence of homosexual behavior is "castration anxiety," the fear, by the male homosexual, of the female genitals. For example, Fenichel writes that homosexual men are terrified of the sight of a partner without a penis because of their own unconscious fear that they might be subject to castration. This is connected with the Oedipus complex, in which the boy is said to be frightened away from his incestuous feelings toward his mother by a feeling that the father will castrate him if he persists in this desire toward his maternal parent. Fenichel writes,

> The sight of female genitals may arouse anxiety in a boy in two ways: (1) The recognition of the fact that there are actually human beings without a penis leads to the conclusion that one might also become such a being; such an observation lends effectiveness to old threats of castration. Or (2) the female genitals, through the connection of castration anxiety with old oral anxieties, may be perceived as a castrating instrument

capable of biting or tearing off the penis. Quite frequently a combination of both types of fear is encountered. (Fenichel, 1945, p. 330.)

The possibility that an individual may not desire sex with women because of castration anxiety cannot be discounted. The notion that all male homosexuals suffer from castration anxiety is patently false, however, because there are a large number of males with an extensive homosexual history—the majority, in fact—who during the same time engage in considerable heterosexual intercourse. That there are many men who are subject to the kind of fear which Fenichel describes is not to be gainsaid here. But we see that this hypothesis, if carried too far, can lead to false conclusions. For example, on the next page, Fenichel states that what these men really want is a "girl with a penis," i.e., they are naturally attracted to women but they are afraid of a penisless object, so they are really looking for a woman who has a penis. Since there are no such creatures, they choose boys. But the boys must have a maximum of girlish and feminine traits. Thus they are attracted to the effeminate homosexual who is the closest approximation to a girl with a penis.

Actually, as a description of homosexual preferences this is simply false. Male homosexuals are most attracted by *masculine* partners and not by effeminate ones. It is clear to any student of the homosexual world that effeminate men are held in much lower esteem than are masculine-looking homosexuals, and it is masculinity rather than girlishness which is most desired in the sexual partners of most male homosexuals.

A complete catalogue of the psychological reasons lying behind homosexual object-choice would take us very far afield, for each individual is different, and the constellation of factors which lead to homosexuality in each particular man is quite diverse. Nevertheless, I would like to mention several other elements in the causation of a homosexual orientation.

One of those most frequently cited is the boy's identification with his mother. According to this explanation, the boy models certain aspects of his behavior after those of the mother (with whom he is usually in closer proximity as a child) rather than the father. One of the results of this may be a desire to enjoy sexual intercourse in the way in which the child imagines the mother does. He wants to play the mother's role in relation to a man. In some cases this leads to the desire to take the receptor role in anal intercourse. If the identification with the mother is strong enough, the boy may develop effeminate traits.

Another result of identification with the mother is that the homosexual male takes as his sexual object younger partners, e.g., adolescent boys, and behaves in some respects toward them as he would have liked his mother to behave toward him. This is what analysts refer to as a narcissistic type of sexual object-choice. In this case, the individual, while choosing the object on the basis of maternal identification, is also identifying with the partner, whom in some sense he regards as a representation of himself. He takes care of the partner and shows tenderness toward him, in some respects like the way in which he imagined or would have liked his mother to behave toward him. Obviously, this latter type of homosexual object-choice can also result from a paternal identification with a desire to behave toward a young man as he would have liked his father to behave toward him. Actually there is virtually no end to the possible combinations of psychodynamics involved in any given case of sexual object-choice, and this statement holds for heterosexual as well as homosexual behavior.

Another type of homosexual orientation results from factors

very similar to those involved in the case of the young man we presented earlier in the present chapter. In this instance the individual has strong angry feelings toward another male, e.g., the father or brother. However, this anger is not very easy to live with since it means making a member of his immediate environment, or someone very close to him, a continual object of hatred, and thus results in introducing a dangerous figure into his interpersonal world. In what is technically known as a reaction formation, he handles this problem by developing "love" for the other person and thus neutralizes the hostility. If this other person is a male this may result in a homosexual orientation, which may persist in later years. This may have other psychological advantages besides the elimination of a hostile figure from the environment. For example, if the individual feels guilt from heterosexual behavior, he can enjoy heterosexual conquest on the part of his brother in a vicarious way. When his love object is successful with women, he not only avoids the competition with him, but also does not have to deal with his own feelings of guilt about heterosexuality.

To some extent, these examples of the psychodynamics of homosexuality are presented only as illustrative. They are certainly not intended to be comprehensive, for we can see that when many factors are involved—as they usually are— there are a large number of possible combinations.

Family Dynamics

A number of writers, among whom Irving Bieber (1962) is eminent, have emphasized a particular family constellation present in male homosexuals. In some sense this is a stereotype, for it clearly applies to some and not to all male homosexuals. And yet it is not without value in understanding the origins of homosexuality, for it points to the fact that the psychodynamics that we have been discussing must have originated in relation to particular kinds of familial patterns present during the early years of the future homosexual.

Bieber's characteristic homosexual-producing mother is over-close and over-intimate with her son. She is very much afraid of losing the son and thus is possessive, and this possessiveness results in a kind of demasculinization of him. She favors that son who is later to become a homosexual over her other children and often over the husband as well, and encourages an alliance with him against the father, so that the son is alienated from masculine identification. She is herself puritanically sexually frigid but, on the other hand, her closeness stimulates the son sexually so that he is aroused and *at the same time* inhibited in the presence of a woman. This is a crucial factor in his later inability to relate sexually to women, for as a child he has to severely repress his over-aroused heterosexual feelings. The son develops a submissiveness and a tendency to worry about displeasing his mother. Often the sleeping arrangements are atypical and the son and mother sleep together until well into adolescence—if not in the same bed, at least in the same room. The result of all this is a severe inhibition of masculinity and assertiveness on the part of the son. This, Bieber feels, is due in large part to an unconscious attempt on the part of the mother to extinguish the son's heterosexuality. Certainly, if this is done, the mother does not lose the boy to other women but retains him as an unconscious incestuous object. If this is, in fact, her psychodynamics, she would also want to desexualize him since, if she has unconscious sexual feelings toward her son, she would not want him to respond sexually to those feelings, because they would be too threatening to her. Even if one does not postulate an unconscious incestuous wish on the part of the mother toward her son, it is clear that there are a lot of women who find in their children the only meaningful relationships in their lives and they often hold the children much too close, well past the time when the child should be going out in the world and making his own new attachments. The "mama's boy" is obviously that kind of boy in large part because the mama wants her boy to stay with her as an interpersonal, if not a sexual, object.

Latent Homosexuality

A term which is used very widely, in fact often bandied about, is "latent homosexuality." If all males have feelings toward both sexes, as Freud held, then all exclusive heterosexuals are latent homosexuals and all exclusive homosexuals are latent heterosexuals. Bisexual men would be the only ones who presumably do not have these two general types of "latent" sexual feelings (although they may have latent incestuous and otherwise sexually repressed feelings). In the previous chapter, we have felt it wise to reject the notion of constitutional bisexuality. What, then, of the concept of latent homosexuality? It seems that while this notion has been subject to abuse, it is one which cannot be discarded, for it *does* point to an obvious factor in the sexual lives of many persons. If it is true that sexual feelings develop in relation to the parents, on a learned basis, and that conscious homosexual feelings do not exist in the majority of adult males because society causes its males to repress them, then they exist, in some sense, in the unconscious. If this is so, as we believe, then very many males have latent homosexual feelings, although we would not want to state unequivocally that 100 percent of all non-homosexual males have unconscious homosexual feelings. Still, there must be a considerable fraction who do, for it is hard to account for a good deal of the hostility toward homosexuals which many heterosexuals display without postulating that they find homosexual males very threatening because of something *within themselves*. If homosexual feelings arise in the way we have hypothesized and then are subject to repression because of social pressure, then Freud was a good deal more correct than we might otherwise believe when we discarded his theory of constitutional bisexuality. What is very clear is that there are a great many men who are struggling with homosexual problems. We will try to show in a later chapter how this struggle may lead to clinical mental illness, and also we want to implicate it in some of the crucial difficulties that overt homosexuals themselves have in the gay world.

Adolescent Peer Relationships: A Vignette

Walter is a 47-year-old business executive. His view of his homosexuality (with which I agree) is that a crucial factor in its development was the problems he had during adolescence with his schoolmates, especially his male peers. He came from a family *not* like those described by Bieber as typical for homosexuality. His mother was the passive parent and was quite devoted to her husband. Walter's relationship with his father was close and, he feels, quite satisfactory. He says his childhood was very happy.

When he entered high school, however, he began to have troubles. He was rather clumsy and never good at athletics, in which he had no interest anyway. (It might be added that neither did his father, so even if his father was a good role model, Walter certainly wouldn't have picked up any such interests from him.) As a result of this disinterest and inability at sports, he became isolated from his age-mates, who all considered athletic interest a *sine qua non* for social acceptance and gave the greatest prestige to athletic stars. As a complicating factor, Walter had a fairly severe case of acne during his early teens, and so was considered unattractive by the good-looking girls at school.

As a result of all this, he began to feel that maybe there was something amiss in his masculinity. He formed a friendship with another outcast who, unlike Walter, had effeminate mannerisms. They finally engaged in some homosexual experiences, which were not at first defined as such, but which they later came to regard as gay. (Unlike most of their classmates, both were interested in reading, and they eventually discovered that there was such a thing as homosexuality. They then had to admit to themselves that they were engaging in homosexual acts.)

From this point in his life, Walter's sexual development took a definitely homosexual course. By the time he got to college he was ready and eager to enter the gay world. He feels that if he had been accepted socially by his high school peers he might have developed in a more "normal" direction. While this cannot be proved, it is hard to imagine that his adolescent problems did not have a profound effect on his sexual orientation.

Social Factors in the Genesis of Homosexuality

In the bulk of this chapter we have been trying to account for homosexual object-choice, the desire for members of one's own sex as sexual partners. There are, however, reasons other than those which are explicitly sexual that cause young men to enter the gay world and participate in homosexual activity. Certainly the phenomenon of male prostitution would indicate that money alone may be a significant factor. Although certain psychoanalysts have claimed that all male prostitutes whose clients are men are "really" homosexual, it appears that most contemporary students of the subject have concluded that there exists a significant number of these male prostitutes who are not basically gay, but who are nevertheless capable of achieving an erection and orgasm if sufficient physical stimulus is applied to the genitals. We do not want to consider hustling at this time; what we want to do is point out certain factors in the modern urban world which lead young men into a homosexual way of life in the relative absence of a strong sexual desire for other men. In discussing these factors, we don't wish to imply that they are somehow mutually exclusive to psychogenic sexual factors, for the two very often combine, especially in those who are bisexually oriented, to produce a homosexual way of life which lasts for a period of at least a few years.

A number of observers, such as Kenneth Keniston (1965), have pointed out the damaging effects of modern urbanized, technological society in producing a serious alienation between persons, especially in the larger cities. This decline in a sense of community between urban Americans has created a powerful impetus toward deviant behavior, for one of the positive virtues to be gained from being deviant is that one gains both a sense of identity and a community of fellows. Being heterosexual does not provide an identity for an alienated, confused modern individual, since everybody is expected to be heterosexual, and this provides about as much of a clue to *who one is* as liking ice cream. To be a homosexual, however, is quite a different matter, for the individual can define himself as a homosexual and can make this identity the center of his own self-concept and of his behavior. At the same time, it makes him a member of a deviant community, and wherever he goes he can find a small group of individuals who will have something in common with him which is very real and very intrinsic to their own being. This is true, of course, for a number of other forms of deviant behavior as well, such as "bohemian" or "hippie" life styles.

Especially if one is young and attractive, being homosexual means belonging to an underground community of fellows which provides one with not only a sense of one's identity, but also with places to go and things to do, even in an otherwise foreign location. In this sense, if the analogy may be pardoned, the homosexual community is like the early Christian communities during the time when Christianity was persecuted by the Romans. When a Christian ventured from his own city to another town, he would immediately look up the Christians in that new locale and would find camaraderie, food, and a place to stay. It is the same for the young homosexual. Before he ventures from his own town to a different city, he will be provided by his home-town friends with a list of gay bars and perhaps with the names of a number of homosexuals whom he can look up. He feels that he belongs to a fraternity of individuals like himself, with whom he has something very basic in common. He feels they will care about him, and in a very real sense he is right. The analogy, of course, ends very abruptly, because unlike the early Christians, who cared for their brothers as persons, the young homosexual will find that his homosexual brothers usually only care for him as a sexual object. Although they may invite him out to dinner and give him a place to stay, when they have satisfied their sexual interest in him, they will likely forget about his existence and his own personal needs.

Still, something is better than nothing, and a shallow community is better than no community at all. Furthermore, there is a very seductive quality about gay life in the large cities which is extremely attractive to the kind of young man who wants to be admired and sought after by other individuals. For in that gay community he can find a kind of attention, from a large number of individuals, which he simply cannot get from a large number of women—certainly not without great effort on his part. Among the individuals who will actively court him, take him out to dinner, buy him presents, and otherwise indicate that to them he is (at least temporarily) a very special person, are people of prominence and wealth. There is no question that, to a number of young men, homosexuality is a way of rising in the socioeconomic scale. The social mobility which is offered to a young man by the homosexual world is much greater than he would find in the heterosexual world, unless he was very lucky indeed. The garage attendant or laundry man will find himself attending elegant cocktail parties in San Francisco's Nob Hill or Pacific Heights. If he is lucky, he will find himself living there, perhaps driving a new sports car or having his way paid through college. These are very powerful inducements, and there are plenty of handsome boys who find themselves caught up in the gay world and engaging in frequent homosexual acts who would otherwise not have a compelling interest in sexual relations with other males. Of course, this is often a form of hustling, and like the street hustler, such a career may end in a commitment to a homosexual way of life, but it may also end by a return to heterosexuality once the young man has achieved the material goals he is after. There is no question, however, that aims which our society considers quite laudable, such as obtaining a higher education, may only be made possible for some persons by their willingness to engage in a homosexual relationship.

The most serious problem which many young men face today is the problem of what to do with their time and how to make their actions meaningful. One of the most attractive features of the gay world, especially in large cities, is that it provides a constant round of activities. There are always bars to visit and parties to go to; there are always new people to meet and go to bed with. There is a certain routine about settling down with one sexual partner which can be entirely obviated by taking up a promiscuous homosexual life. In spite of the increasing availability of girls as sexual partners, there is nothing to compare with the ready availability of other males to the attractive young homosexual. The whole scene is very seductive and glamorous, especially when one has first entered it. It is a constant source of meaning and one's self-esteem is continually buoyed up.

Since virtually the sole criterion of value in the homosexual world is physical attractiveness, being young and handsome in gay life is like being a millionaire in a community where wealth is the only criterion of value.

9

○
● ●

The Disease Concept
of Homosexuality

At the present time, the most fashionable view of a homosexually oriented object-choice is that it is a mental illness or a symptom of mental illness. Perhaps the most influential exponent of this view today is the New York psychoanalyst Irving Bieber. Bieber's book (1962) is a strange mixture of astute clinical observation and the worst kind of pseudoscience. He interviewed a group of his psychoanalytic colleagues and elicited from them reports about patients they had treated in psychoanalysis. He compared the case histories of 106 male homosexuals and 100 male heterosexuals treated by these colleagues. Bieber starts out with the assumption that homosexuality is a mental illness and finds, perhaps not surprisingly, that his clinical findings support his assumption! There are actually few new ideas in the book about the origins of homosexual object-choice; most of Bieber's conceptualizations had already been published in earlier psychoanalytic writings. What *is* new is the scientistic cast which Bieber presents to his readers. He subjects the data supplied by his colleagues to statistical analysis, and the book is replete with tables, charts, numerical terminology, and similar signs of scientific pretension. However, none of these quantitative devices can disguise the fact that such methodological analysis cannot possibly yield more from the data than is there to begin with. In other words, subjecting the responses of Bieber's colleagues to statistical analysis does not obviate the fact that these responses derive from a clinical procedure (psychoanalysis) which yields results which are still to a large extent speculative, and which represent primarily the original, very insightful, theoretical assumptions of the early analysts.

In the previous chapter, I have used Bieber's explanation of the family dynamics involved in the production of some forms of homosexuality to point to one possible factor in the genesis of this form of behavior. The trouble with Bieber's book is not that it contains nothing useful, but that the claims he makes for his findings are so inappropriate that they make one wonder from where such claims arise. On reading his book, I think it becomes obvious that his claims about homosexuality being an illness do not come from the data itself. These claims are, rather, the result of a prior assumption that Bieber and his collaborators have agreed upon. Having already decided that homosexuality is an illness, they have then studied the clinical case histories to document that assumption. As a result of their study, they have "concluded" that they were right all along, i.e., that homosexuality is indeed an illness.

The flaws in Bieber's method are twofold: first, any inquiry that seeks to use only one kind of data to the exclusion of other data in order to substantiate a preconceived conclusion is not scientific; second, such data which do seem to support the preconceived conclusion may also be used, and perhaps even more advantageously, to support many other conclusions which the investigator has rejected on no other grounds than his prejudice. That individuals who come to psychoanalysts for treatment are usually mentally ill is a tautology—unless we can offer another explanation for their presence. Given this fact, it is reasonable to assume that a competent psychiatrist will diagnose most of his clients in one way or another as mentally ill. One would, therefore, expect that all homosexuals treated by psychiatrists are found to be mentally ill. How a psychiatrist can conclude from this fact that *all* homosexuals are mentally ill remains something of a mystery, and yet it is done all the time. The Philadelphia psychiatrist Samuel B. Hadden recently published an article in *Harper's* (March, 1967) in which he wrote, "In my observation, homosexuals are deeply troubled people . . . from earliest childhood none of the homosexuals I have known have been truly psychologically healthy individuals" (pp. 107, 114). What always appears most curious to me is that psychiatrists such as Bieber and Hadden can write this kind of thing with a straight face. When Hadden tells us that none of the homosexuals he has known are mentally healthy, the logical conclusion is that he has never known any mentally healthy homosexuals. But this is not the conclusion *he* draws. Instead, he comes to the conclusion that there *are* no mentally healthy homosexuals—which is quite another matter.

But since he is forming dogmatic conclusions on the basis of his clinical experience alone, one can only suggest to him that he has no idea of what scientific method is all about. To put it in more technical terminology, Bieber and Hadden are claiming representativeness for a particular sample of a certain social group which is, in fact, not necessarily representative of that group. Homosexuals seen in psychiatric treatment are no more representative of homosexuals in the general population than are Jews seen in psychiatric treatment representative of all Jews. If I had to judge solely from my own psychiatric practice, I would have come to the same conclusions as Bieber and Hadden. None of the homosexuals I have treated has been mentally healthy; they were all sick. What I have refused to do, however, is to assume that my patients were the only kind of homosexuals that there are. It seemed to me quite obvious that they were not a representative or random sample of the general homosexual population.

I do not claim to be the first one to make this methodological critique of psychiatric writings on homosexuality. The psychoanalyst Ernest van den Haag wrote the following:

> To be sure, homosexual behavior often is a symptom or part of illness; so is heterosexual behavior. (I am reminded of a colleague who reiterated "all my homosexual patients are quite sick"—to which I finally replied "so are all my heterosexual patients." As our culture has absorbed analysis, analysts have become culture-bound. It seems a questionable gain.)
>
> Many homosexuals are neurotic or psychotic and seek the help of analysts, as do many heterosexuals. It does not follow that homosexuality itself is an illness—that it is always associated with clinical symptoms . . . of disturbance. (1963, p. 297.)

I might only add that van den Haag and I are not alone in taking this position in opposition to a large number of our colleagues. In his famous letter to the mother of an American homosexual, written on April 9, 1935, Freud wrote that homosexuality cannot be classified as an illness. In one of the most influential books published during the twentieth century, *Three Essays on the Theory of Sexuality*, Freud wrote the following:

> Inversion is found in people who exhibit no other serious deviations from the normal. It is similarly found in people whose efficiency is unimpaired, and who are indeed distinguished by specially high intellectual development and ethical culture. (1925, p. 17.)

One of the reasons that I decided to do an ethnographic, community, or non-clinical study of homosexuals was because I felt that the homosexuals whom I was seeing in treatment were not representative of the general homosexual population. In the course of this work, one of the questions I was interested in answering was: are there a significant number of homosexuals who, by reasonable clinical criteria, cannot be considered mentally ill? The answer which I have found to this question is unequivocally in the affirmative. I have interviewed numerous men (and in many cases have extensive corroborating data from their friends and associates) who simply cannot be diagnosed mentally ill on the basis of any clinical psychiatric criteria known to me. My own observations, therefore, provide more evidence to support Freud's statements quoted above.

But the reader does not need to take my word, van den Haag's word, or even Freud's word on this matter. There are more rigorous studies recently made which come to the same conclusion. In an investigation reported in the *British Medical Journal* in 1957, two English psychiatrists, Desmond Curran and Denis Parr, studied 100 cases seen in consultation in their private psychiatric practice. Of these 100 homosexual men, 30 came because of some difficulty with the law and 25 came because they were troubled by their propensity toward socially unacceptable behavior. The rest came for other reasons, including standard psychiatric problems. Curran and Parr found that only 49 percent of these homosexuals showed significant psychiatric abnormalities, and that the abnormalities manifested were usually minimal. This means that, if one were to examine a psychiatrist's initial psychiatric evaluations of a sample of all individuals who come to his attention, rather than to study those patients who have been placed in extensive psychiatric treatment, one would find that the majority of those who are homosexual (which, incidentally, Curran and Parr found to be 5 percent of all their male patients over the age of 16) "were considered to be free from gross personality disorder, neurosis, or psychosis during their adult lives" (p. 797). If Bieber or Hadden had seen these patients, they would surely have diagnosed them as mentally ill, since they have already assumed that homosexuality is an illness. They would then have placed the patients in treatment and found a psychiatric label for them.

At this point we must raise very briefly the whole question of the nature of mental illness. This is a very large and difficult subject and one which itself has an extensive literature. What is, I think, clear is that the diagnosis of mental illness is the result of a process of social definition and that certain individuals in society, usually psychiatrists, are granted the prerogative of making this definition. The standard which the psychiatrist has to use is determined by the general consensus among the community of his colleagues. Thus, he can, as is presently the case, define homosexuality *per se* as a mental illness merely because a large number of his colleagues have agreed that it is so. On the other hand, since there is no universal agreement about the matter, it is possible to hold a minority point of view, such as the view I hold. I maintain that homosexuality in itself does not necessarily indicate mental illness. The question is partly definitional and partly empirical. The definitional question is: do we want to say that a sexual preference for one's own sex is, by itself, either a mental illness or a symptom of an illness? This is a question which cannot altogether be solved by adducing scientific evidence, since it is basically a matter of attaching a particular label (mental illness) to a particular kind of sexual object-choice (homosexual). For those who elect to attach this label, the sexual object-choice in itself is sufficient ground for doing so, and no other evidence need be adduced.

As a matter of fact, the people who write on this subject are generally unclear as to what they mean, and the reader is very often confused or misled when he is finished reading what they have to say. They make two separate claims: (1) that homosexual behavior or preference is *itself* an illness; and (2) that homosexual behavior or preference is always associated with *other* clinical symptoms. The first claim, as we have indicated, is a matter of definition. The second claim is capable of empirical test. It has actually been empirically refuted.

The classic study which has refuted this notion was done by U.C.L.A. psychologist Evelyn Hooker and published in 1957. Hooker found 30 homosexuals whom she felt were reasonably well adjusted and were not in treatment. She obtained these men, to a large extent, with the assistance of the Mattachine Society, "an organization which has as its stated purpose the development of a homosexual ethic in order to better integrate the homosexual into society" (Hooker, 1957, p. 19). She then obtained 30 heterosexual men who were matched for age, education, and IQ with the homosexual subjects. Hooker then gave these 60 men a battery of psychological tests, including the Rorschach, the TAT, and the MATS, and obtained considerable information on their life histories. She then submitted this material for analysis to several of her colleagues, who did not know which of the tests had been given to the homosexual men and which to the heterosexual men; therefore, they analyzed the tests "blind." Hooker's general conclusion from the results of these analyses, made by clinicians who did not know the sexual orientation of the subjects in the study, was that there is no inherent connection between homosexual orientation and clinical symptoms of mental illness. She stated that "Homosexuality as a clinical entity does not exist. Its forms are as varied as are those of heterosexuality. Homosexuality may be a deviation in sexual pattern which is in the normal range, psychologically" (*ibid.*, p. 30). This conclusion is based on the fact that the clinicians who read the tests were unable to distinguish between the two groups. Nor was there any evidence that the homosexual group had a higher degree of pathology than the heterosexual group. When a sensitive clinical instrument, such as the Rorschach, was used, the conclusions were the same as those reached by Curran and Parr, by Freud, by van den Haag, and by myself, namely, that there certainly exists a significant number of homosexual men who are not mentally ill by any clinical criteria.

If all this evidence is not to be discounted, then it is clear that the overt male homosexual is not necessarily subject to clinical symptoms of illness, to neurotic or psychotic disturbance. There are, of course, a number of questions which remain unanswered. One of them is: if one could get a random sample of the homosexual population and a random sample of the heterosexual population, and one could compare these two groups, would there be any higher incidence of mental disturbance in the homosexual group? This is indeed a very interesting question, but there exists no answer to it, because there is no feasible way of getting a random sample of the homosexual population, since it is an occult population. Even if one could get such a sample, one would run into extremely serious problems in the application of clinical criteria to these individuals. It would be incumbent upon those doing the research to do what Hooker did, namely, to find some way of keeping the clinical judges from knowing the sexual object-choice of the individuals whose clinical histories they were studying. This is because so many clinicians of the Bieber or Hadden persuasion would be immediately prejudiced by such knowledge. At any rate, these questions are all very hypothetical because at present there does not seem to be any way to get a random sample of this kind of population. The only way in which such a sample might be approached is through a very large-scale study of the American population as a whole, such as was done by Kinsey and his associates. It may be added, somewhat parenthetically, that it might very well be worth while at this time to attempt to re-do certain aspects of Kinsey's original studies asking some questions he did not, and using some of the techniques which he did not, such as a probability sample. But this is altogether another matter.

Perhaps the reader may be somewhat perplexed by the foregoing content of this chapter, for in Chapter 8, when discussing the dynamics which may lead to a homosexual adjustment, we described a number of possible routes to a homosexual orientation, all of which were quite obviously pathologic, e.g., the individual who performs fellatio on a serviceman in order to incorporate his imputed masculinity. Again, then, let me say that these "symbolic" routes to homosexuality, while the most vivid, the easiest to describe, and the easiest for the reader to remember, are not the only routes which individuals may take. The fact that the child develops his sexual feelings in relation to the people in his immediate environment, including his male parent and his female parent, postulates a possibility that he might develop homosexual feelings which do *not* involve the kinds of symbolic mechanisms, e.g., the "sacramental feast," which we have described earlier. I want to repeat here again what was said in the previous chapter, namely, that such explanations cover only *some* of the cases. What percentage of cases they cover is altogether unknown. Claims, such as those made by certain psychoanalysts, that *all* homosexuals are afraid of female genitals (Bieber), have castration anxiety (Fenichel), etc., must be discounted on at least two grounds. In the first place, they do not account for the enormous number of men who are able to have satisfactory sexual relations with women *and* satisfactory sexual relations with men during the same period of time in their lives. Second, they are based on highly questionable generalizations from the study of certain psychoanalytic patients. While I would not question these explanations as applied to these particular patients, to make the claim that they apply uniformly to all male homosexuals is an example of the kind of unwarranted generalizations for which psychoanalysts have been justifiably criticized for many years. While I am firmly of the opinion that Freud's contribution to the study of man is one of the truly signal achievements in the history of human thought, I do not believe that his is the only approach to the investigation of human behavior or that generalizations derived from the study of patients in psychoanalysis can be indiscriminately applied to individuals outside the analytic consulting room.

10

Promiscuity and the Problem of Intimacy

The most serious problem for those who live in the gay world is the great difficulty they have in establishing stable paired relationships with each other. In calling attention to this problem, I would like to point out that my emphasis on it does not stem primarily from my own personal belief that such relationships are desirable (though I would readily admit to such a prejudice), but rather from the information conveyed by the homosexual men themselves. Although there are some exceptions, in general they are very unhappy about the grave difficulties which inhibit the formation of stable

166

relationships. They are continually looking for more permanence in their socio-sexual lives and are all too often unable to find it.

We must now attempt an explanation of the difficulties which interfere with the development of intimacy between two homosexual males. In doing so, we shall take as our comparative groups not only heterosexual couples but also female homosexual couples, who have much less difficulty than homosexual males in the formation of stable relationships. It is the general consensus of those few investigators who have studied the female homosexual community, as well as psychiatrists who have worked with female homosexuals, that these women form lasting ties of intimacy much more commonly and much more easily than do male homosexuals. Their public activities are significantly different from the public behavior of homosexual men, as described in earlier chapters. They do not cruise streets or parks or lavatories. There are a few lesbian bars, but they are very small in proportion both to the number of male homosexual bars and to the total lesbian population. Furthermore, female homosexuals do not use the bars in the same way that men do. They rarely pick up partners for one-night stands but, rather, engage in a kind of courtship ritual which is very much like that of heterosexual couples. That is, they typically become socially acquainted with one another first, then go out on dates, and tend to leave the sexual involvement to a later stage in the relationship. This sequence is quite unlike that of the males, who usually begin potential sexual relationships with an immediate sexual encounter.

There is no question—regardless of what one might say about the hypothesized increasing tendency toward "sexual freedom" in our society, in general—that male homosexual relationships have a different character than those of either heterosexual couples or lesbians. They tend to be characterized by extreme promiscuity and what I earlier called sex fetishization, and it is this finding that we want to explain, partly out of scientific curiosity but, more importantly, because this situation is of serious concern to the actors themselves in this unhappy drama. They often feel caught up in the web of promiscuity and instability and wish there were some way they could escape from it.

Differences in Sexual Response
between Males and Females

It is clear that a very important factor in the problem of promiscuity is due to the fact that the male homosexual relationship is a relationship involving two males. This may sound like a tautology, but it is not. One certain, crucial element in the answer to the dilemma lies in the fact that, regardless of all psychological and cultural determinants, a relationship involving sex between two males does not have the same character as one involving two females or a male and female. In the Kinsey volume *Sexual Behavior in the Human Female* (1953), the sixteenth chapter (Psychologic Factors in Sexual Response) contains much fascinating data which bear on this question:

> Among all peoples, everywhere in the world, it is understood that the male is more likely than the female to desire sexual relations with a variety of partners. It is pointed out that the female has a greater capacity for being faithful to a single partner, that she is more likely to consider that she has a greater responsibility than the male has in maintaining the home and in caring for the offspring of any sexual relationship, and that she is generally more inclined to consider the moral implications of her sexual behavior. But it seems probable that these char-

acteristics depend upon the fact that the female is less often aroused, as the average male is aroused, by the idea of promiscuity. (P. 682.)

Kinsey and his collaborators have assembled a great deal of evidence which indicates that males and females respond quite differently, psychologically, to sexual stimuli. One of the central differences is that males are much more responsive to visual stimuli than are females. In other words, they become sexually aroused *before* they make any physical contact with their potential partner, whereas females tend to become aroused only after this contact has been made. This fundamental difference, which appears to hold widely in the animal kingdom as well as in humans, is a great impetus to promiscuity, for it means that visual contact alone can, for the male, provide the impetus to a sexual encounter, whereas a female will be relatively unaroused by such stimuli.

As part of the evidence for this difference, it should be pointed out that pornography is an enterprise that functions almost exclusively for male customers. Whether the material be visual (drawings, photographs, motion pictures, etc.) or literary, men are almost exclusively the consumers of such material. This is true whether the material caters to a heterosexual or a homosexual audience, and for all combinations of actors in a pornographic plot. For example, there are hundreds of novels with a lesbian theme now available in paperback. These are, almost without exception, written for the male heterosexual audience. Female homosexuals are not sexually aroused by reading such material, but male heterosexuals are. Physique magazines, which are the "male" counterpart of the "girlie" magazines, and which show young men in various stages of undress, are produced entirely for the male homosexual audience. Heterosexual women are typically not interested in such material. Women generally do not become erotically aroused by nude photographs, whether of men or of other women, regardless of their sexual orientation.

Males seem much more directly interested in the genitals than are females. They are much more often sexually aroused by the sight of genitalia, either male or female, and much more frequently initiate a sexual relationship through some genital exposure or genital manipulation. Some of the focus on sexual organs which takes place in homosexual relations must be attributed simply to the fact that two males are involved, for some of the criticisms that are made against homosexual men for focusing on the genitalia are very similar to those which heterosexual women make about their husbands for being excessively interested in genital contact and an immediate genital union. It is a very good question to ask to what extent these differences result from biological and to what extent from cultural factors. There is a good deal of evidence that the distinctions we have noted between males and females in our own culture are present widely across varied cultures and are to be found in other species of mammals. As Kinsey writes:

> The males of practically all infra-human species may become aroused when they observe other animals in sexual activity. Of this fact farmers, animal breeders, scientists experimenting with laboratory animals, and many persons who have kept household pets are abundantly aware. The females of the infra-human species less often show such sympathetic responses when they observe other animals in sexual activity. These data suggest that human females are more often inclined to accept the social proprieties because they are stimulated psychologically and respond sympathetically less often than most males do. (*Ibid.,* pp. 661–62.)

The Kinsey data, especially when viewed in the context of studies of infra-human mammals, strongly suggest that the factors which account for these differences go beyond the cultural and involve some basic biological differences in sexual response between males and females.

We must at this point, however, reintroduce a distinction made earlier, between a tendency toward promiscuity and an inability or severe difficulty in forming lasting paired relationships. The psychologic differences between males and females in the nature of erotic response that we have discussed account for a tendency toward promiscuity, to at least a very great extent. However, their ability to account for the severe problems that homosexual males have in forming and maintaining relationships of paired intimacy is less satisfactory. If the (very likely biological) tendency toward promiscuity among males precluded their forming stable socio-sexual relationships, then heterosexual males would be unable to form alliances with females. Thus, even though females might wish to form such alliances, they would be much more tenuous than they presently appear to be—even granting our high divorce rate. I think we must take the tendency toward promiscuity into account as a real factor which undoubtedly makes more difficult the formation of stable alliances between homosexual males, but we must not overweigh it or confuse it with the other factors which contribute to this problem.

Psychodynamic Factors

One of the fascinating questions which remain unanswered in the study of homosexual life is to what extent homosexuals are produced by pathogenic or traumatic factors in their early years. As I have argued in previous chapters, the evidence indicates that while some of them are produced by such factors, not all of them are, and the evidence also clearly shows that not all homosexuals can be considered mentally ill or psychologically abnormal. Nevertheless, it is reasonable to conclude that in a society such as ours, which strongly condemns such kinds of behavior and sexual orientation, there is a higher percentage of psychologically disturbed individuals in the homosexual than in the heterosexual categories. There is really no solid evidence on this question, but my own judgment, based on general theoretical considerations about the formation of deviant patterns, and also on my observation of the homosexual world, leads me to believe that this is probably the case.

I do have the definite feeling that while there are many mentally healthy homosexual males, there is a greater tendency toward mental illness in the homosexual than in the heterosexual world. Since students of the epidemiology of mental illness cannot at present agree on criteria for assessing the mental health of non-deviant populations, it seems very unlikely that we will arrive at a valid assessment of the mental health of an occult deviant community, such as the homosexual, within the near future. Therefore we will have to rely on such impressionistic evidence.

We also should consider, however, some general theoretical notions abut the formation of deviant behavior. In any given society, certain patterns of perception, thought, and action are encouraged and certain others are discouraged. The rewards of following the accepted mode of behavior, as well as the punishments for deviant conduct, are sufficient to provide a fairly adequate general explanation for socially normative behavior. Hence, while the explanation of *all* behavior is certainly a scientific problem, the explanation of deviant behavior is a problem of a different kind, for it does not necessarily or always require an explanation of the more general question, i.e., the formation of social behavior as a whole. To some extent, therefore, the problem is one of explaining why individuals do *not* follow the given cultural pattern. The answer must be, in part, that they do not follow this cultural pattern because they are *unable* to do so. Many homosexual men are homosexual precisely because they are unable to be heterosexual, for one reason or another. They may indeed be afraid of the female genitals, or they may be afraid of a lasting, close relationship with another person, which is much more likely to arise from a heterosexual affair than from a homosexual one. My argument against the generalizations made by Fenichel and Bieber is not that their theoretical explanations for the origins of homosexual object-choice do not apply to many homosexuals but, rather, that they do not apply to *all* such men.

What I am trying to indicate is that the psychodynamic factors which we have previously described in accounting for the origins of homosexual object-choice must, to some extent, inevitably account also for the inability to form stable relationships. For example, if an individual becomes homosexual because he feels that he is insufficiently masculine, and his dominating fantasy is that if he sucks the penis of another man he will incorporate that man's masculinity into his own self, then his ability to form a stable relationship may be permanently impaired. What he will discover is that the act of fellatio does *not* provide the increased sense of masculinity which he had thought it would. He is not, of course, *aware* of the unconscious goal of his deviant act. He is looking for something, but he does not know what he is looking for. When he fails to find satisfaction, he is inclined to repeat the act with another partner in a compulsive attempt to obtain what he unconsciously feels to be so necessary to his well-being. Consequently, he has a tendency to repeat the act of fellatio on successive individuals, but is unable to say why he does not wish to repeat the act with the same individual more than once. Actually, once he has not found what he wanted, he no longer has any interest in that partner, since the interest was originally determined by a need altogether out of awareness of his conscious mind.

At the same time, such individuals, i.e., those whose route into homosexual patterns is quite pathologic, are the very individuals for whom stable interpersonal relations would be a problem, even if their sexual orientation is not taken into account. This is because these individuals chronically suffer from a low sense of their own worth as persons and from a myriad of psychological difficulties which revolve around their relations to other people. It is generally accepted in psychiatry today that the origins of mental illness are intimately connected with difficulties in interpersonal relations. Thus, if there is a higher incidence of pathology among the homosexual population, as we have suggested, we would expect that there would be a higher degree of promiscuity, simply because of this. We would expect that this tendency toward promiscuity would, unlike the biological tendency we have described above, be directly correlated not only with promiscuity as such but also with an inability to form lasting relationships with another person which involve that degree of closeness which a paired sexual relationship implies.

Social and Cultural Factors

The term "gay marriage" is one which is used in the homosexual world to describe paired relationships which last for a period of time. If one reflects upon this term, one can immediately see that there are hosts of powerful social forces which promote the stability of heterosexual marriages that are not present to encourage a similar stability between homosexual partners. Heterosexual marriages are institutionalized by church and state. Heterosexual couples fit into society in numerous ways, both obvious and subtle, in which homosexual couples cannot partake. It is simply not prudent for many men to become involved in a living relationship with each other, for this would immediately throw suspicion on their sexual orientation. Furthermore, the partner in a gay marriage cannot participate in social activities in the straight world which are open to the wife of a heterosexual male. A businessman, for example, cannot take his young lover to a dinner given by his firm at the country club. Relations with one's family may become severely strained if the family finds out that one is living with another man. This is especially problematic if there is a discrepancy in the ages of the partners. Two men in their 20's may well get away with pretending they are simply roommates living in an apartment in the big city together in order to conserve funds. If, however, a fairly well-to-do professional man of 40 takes a house in a suburb with an attractive 22-year-old college student, the credulity of family and associates alike is bound to be strained.

Thus, questions about the nature of the relationship are likely to arise if two men are living together, especially over a period of time. Interestingly enough, such questions arise much less frequently when two women live together, for this is considered to be a much more acceptable pattern of life in our society. Here we have a very important clue to one of the reasons for the distinction between the ability of males and females who are homosexually oriented to form stable relationships. Society puts much less of a burden on a lesbian than on a male homosexual couple. It is much less likely to suspect a sexual involvement between two women who are living together or who are known to be (at least socially) intimate. It might be noted in this connection that women are permitted to do things that among men would immediately raise the suspicion of homosexuality. For example, women are permitted to embrace, to kiss, and to dance in public. Anyone who has watched a teenage dance show on television will note that girls in late adolescence dance with each other, whereas such behavior would be unthinkable between boys. It might be noted, in this regard, that the current reform of the criminal law in England, which now allows homosexual relations between consenting adults in private, does not need to take lesbians into consideration, simply because lesbian practices were never illegal in the first place.

These considerations lead us to what I consider to be perhaps the most significant factor involved in the problem of intimacy between male homosexuals, namely, the social prohibition against such intimacy, i.e., the social prohibition against homosexuality. To put the matter in its *most* simple terms, the reason that males who are homosexually inclined cannot form stable relations with each other is that society does not want them to.

The mechanism by which this social prohibition operates is the following: Closeness between men is considered a sign of something wrong with the individuals involved. Unlike closeness between women, which is socially acceptable and certainly casts no doubt on the "femininity" of the two women, closeness between men is thought of as indicating a fault in the masculinity of the two individuals. When such closeness is considered (at some level) in the individual's mind, he immediately defines himself as sissy, faggot, degenerate, etc. The crucial fact about this kind of socially prohibited behavior is that the mechanism of its repression involves the individual incorporating into his own conscience the prohibition against such a form of closeness. At this point the reader may ask, how is it possible, then, that such individuals can engage in sexual relations with other males? The answer to this seems to be that the sexual arousal provides sufficient impetus to overcome the social prohibition against genital contact, but that it does *not* provide sufficient stimulus to overcome the prohibition against intimacy. To overcome this second kind of condemnation would require a kind of freedom from social constraint that is not really to be expected, except in a few cases. That this kind of freedom does occur from time to time raises very interesting theoretical questions, to which we need not address ourselves right here. What we want to point out now is that the majority of homosexual men cannot overcome this social prohibition.

Another way of saying what we have here discussed is that the same social forces which act to prevent most males from becoming homosexual reach into the lives of those that *do* become homosexual and prevent them from developing closeness in a sexual relationship with another man. It seems reasonable to assume that the social forces do not simply stop having profound effects once an individual has developed a homosexual orientation, but rather that they affect the character of that individual's life in other ways. What they do is give the individual a sense that his homosexual behavior is morally wrong, and also that, therefore, his partner is bad. How then is he expected to develop a warm, intimate relationship with a partner whom he unconsciously devalues as a person for engaging in acts with him which he defines as degraded?

Furthermore, there is another side to this coin. The homosexual's own self-concept cannot easily commit him to being any more of a homosexual than is required by the sexual drive itself. To put the matter in another way: it is one thing to cruise the park, pick up a guy, take him home, have sex, never see the partner again, and forget the whole thing. It is another thing to commit oneself to a living relationship with another man in which, 24 hours a day, one is reminded of one's homosexuality by the presence of the other person in one's life. This requires a greater effort in overcoming the social barriers toward homosexual feelings and this is an effort that it is simply not possible for many homosexuals to make. The feelings of guilt—conscious or unconscious—produced by the involvement in homosexual acts, serve to contaminate the relationship and prevent the possibility of its developing into one of warm intimacy.

What is fundamentally wrong with the conventional disease concept of homosexuality is not that there is no connection between homosexuality and pathology, for there is, in fact, such a link. What is incorrect is that all the phenomena of gay life are analyzed in terms of individual pathology, as if there were no social forces acting upon the homosexual. The problem of paired intimacy, which in my judgment is *the central problem* of the gay world, is a problem which cannot meaningfully be understood without considering the social context in which it occurs. It is this failure to consider the social milieu in which the gay world is situated, namely, the hostile character of the surrounding non-homosexual world, that accounts for the simplistic explanations of so much current analysis of the problem.

We are now beginning to realize that social forces have an influence on all kinds of phenomena which we have hitherto analyzed in individual terms. We are beginning to understand, for example, that even physical illness such as heart disease and cancer may be influenced by sociological factors and that such illnesses vary in different parts of the population, in different socioeconomic and ethnic groups. If this be the case, as is plainly indicated by recent studies, then it ought to be clear that the relationship of the homosexual to a larger hostile society must have profound effects on his life which go considerably beyond the legal and social dangers of exposure. It is certainly very clear that one of the reasons for promiscuity is that to some extent, and in many cases, it provides anonymity, for if the partner is not known, then no follow-up of the relationship is possible. If a prominent individual has sex with another man in the park and no non-sexual contact is made, then there is less likelihood that he may be found out. In other words, the need to manage information about one's deviant activity leads to much of the anonymous promiscuity of the gay world.

I want to take the analysis to a deeper level and indicate that actually embedded in the individual's concept of himself is the idea that his homosexual proclivities are bad and that to establish a relationship with another man is carrying these proclivities to a worse extreme. Thus, the instability of relationships which is frequently used as grounds for condemnation of homosexuals is, in fact, the very product of this condemnation. There is thus, to say the least, a strange irony in homosexuals being accused of not forming stable relationships, when it is the social prohibitions they suffer which largely prevent them from becoming involved in such relationships.

11

∴

Dread of Homosexuality

If the reader will grant that the analysis of the gay world presented in the foregoing pages is correct, he will most likely wonder as to the origins of this problem. The gay world, in many respects, is a bad scene, and it is so because of the way homosexuals and homosexuality are treated by the straight world. We could, of course, have spent a great many pages detailing accounts of frank persecution of homosexuals: rejection by their families, dismissals by employers, brutal treatment by law enforcement agencies, etc. The reason we have not done so is that we have had to assume, in a book which attempted to explore the more subtle aspects of the problems of the gay world, the reader would already be sophisticated enough about the ways in which an outcast group can be, and is being, persecuted, so that he would find a detailed accounting of gross inhumanity toward homosexuals to be unnecessary. Perhaps it was wrong to focus on the more subtle problem of relationships between homosexual men themselves; it seems, however, on the basis of my own research, that this is the central problem in the gay world and that it is therefore both scientifically the most interesting and socially the most significant question.

Nevertheless, as we have pointed out, the relation between this problem and the general persecution of homosexuals by society is a very intimate and inextricably connected one. The problem of intimacy between homosexual males is in very large part a product of that very same social repression which leads employers to fire certain of their workers when they discover, or even suspect, that they are gay.

What we are confronted with is a pervasive characteristic of contemporary Western culture, namely, a dread of homosexuality. This dread, which is in large part unconscious, is intimately tied to widely held notions about the nature of masculinity and to what males are and are not permitted in the way of behavior and feelings. When it comes to understanding this dread of homosexuality we owe a very great debt to Freud, for it is his explanation which makes the most sense. Freud held that all individuals had sexual feelings toward members of their same sex, but that these had to be repressed in our society. Therefore, the dread of homosexuality is a result of, and derives its tremendous force from, the wishes for homosexual expression which are present in our unconscious minds. In other words, the fear is intimately connected with the wish, and the wish is only repressed because of the dread which is conjured up by the social taboo. The price, in short, for the repression of homosexual feelings is a very high one.

This price is paid in a very tragic way by those males who *are* able to overcome the repression against homosexual feelings. They pay for it in their inability to mix love and sex, by their isolation of sex from the other parts of their lives, and by their own conscious and unconscious feelings of guilt about their sexual activities. As anyone who saw the play *Tea and Sympathy* will remember, this price is also paid by very many heterosexual males who go through terrible agonies concerning their own masculinity, simply because they are in some ways unable to live up to a stereotype of what a "he-man" ought to be like. (One of the real benefits that will hopefully be derived from the "hippie" movement is that the stereotype of masculinity which has dominated American culture for so long and which has been the source of great unhappiness for so many of those who are unable to live up to it—even though they be basically heterosexual—will be considerably diminished, and a male's sexual and personal identity will no longer be threatened if he likes flowers or cares about the texture of his clothes or likes to wear his hair long, etc.)

The Schreber Case

In 1911, Freud wrote an analysis of the published memoirs of Dr. Daniel Paul Schreber, who was formerly an appellate court judge in Dresden. Schreber's book was published in 1903 as *Memoirs of a Neurotic*, and Freud based his general theory of paranoid delusions upon the analysis of this case. It is unnecessary for us to repeat the train of thought which led to Freud's conclusions, since Freud's article is widely available and the reader may review it for himself. For our purposes, it will suffice to look at Freud's conclusions. Freud held that delusions of persecution arise because of repressed homosexual wishes. The mechanism by which Freud believed this to occur was the following: The individual felt positive, sexually charged feelings toward another male—"I love him." But this feeling he was unable to bear because of the homosexual dread in the culture. By means of a combination of defense mechanisms, the individual turns this feeling upside down, into a more acceptable feeling—"I hate him." But, in order to justify this and allow himself to feel that his antagonism is soundly based, the individual projects the hate onto the other person and says—"He hates me."

Freud did not say that all paranoid schizophrenia was due to unconscious homosexuality. As a matter of fact, he made a rather sharp distinction between paranoid delusions and schizophrenia—a distinction which was common in his day but is no longer recognized by psychiatrists at the present time. He did say, however, that many cases of paranoia could be analyzed in this way and are found to be a result of repressed homosexual wishes. It seems to me that whether or not one agrees entirely with Freud's analysis of the Schreber case, he has here given us another brilliant insight into the nature of mental illness. What he has told us in this case is of lasting value, for we now know that the kind of repressed feelings that led to Dr. Schreber's paranoia are implicated in other cases of paranoia and also in other forms of schizophrenia.

My own interpretation would be that Freud was substantially correct, although I would want to revise some of his theoretical speculations about the origins of this mental illness. What I would want to say is that such individuals have a fairly weak ego to begin with, so that they are already prone to mental disturbance. At the same time, they have a very deep dread of homosexuality, which is intimately connected with strong homosexual wishes. This leads to a potentially explosive situation, for they may at any time encounter an individual who stirs up these very strong feelings. When this encounter takes place they may very well be in a psychological position, for many possible reasons, in which they are unable to handle their feelings. The repressed feelings overwhelm the ego and the individual becomes psychotic. Thus, the dread of homosexuality can literally drive a person crazy. This understanding is what Freud contributed by his brilliant analysis of the Schreber case and, in spite of reservations that might be made about some of Freud's theoretical presuppositions, such as his notion of inherited bisexual drives, his basic understanding of the case still holds. And it holds, moreover, not only for paranoia, but also for much of schizophrenia as well, for we no longer accept the sharp demarcation that was current in the psychiatric thought of his time between these two disease entities. In my own clinical experience, dread of homosexuality can be implicated in the cause of numerous psychotic breaks, as well as all kinds of anxiety states and schizophrenic panics. Our own society, which has thwarted attempts of those homosexual males who are involved in the gay world to form stable relationships with one another, is the same society which has literally driven people insane by its refusal to let them come into conscious contact with their feelings toward other members of their own sex.

Let me cite an example of this: In psychiatric practice, I once treated a 24-year-old married man who had no history whatever of homosexual activity or interests. He flatly denied any such feelings. Nevertheless, he had recently had a schizophrenic break, in which he had hallucinations of strange voices accusing him of being "queer." We immediately commenced a course of psychotherapy. What we found out is that his firm had recently hired an attractive young man with whom he was assigned to work. He developed strong unconscious homosexual feelings toward this man and was simply not able to accept them. As a result, he became profoundly confused as to his sexual identity and developed a psychosis. When this became clarified during the course of treatment the problem was markedly improved. He did not, of course, become homosexual or have an affair with this guy. But he did finally accept the fact that he had had homosexual impulses and that these were not so terrible (or rare) as he had imagined. Ultimately, he could accept them without thinking of himself as some form of degenerate.

It is this kind of self-knowledge that our society makes so difficult for men to acquire, and hence, actually induces psychosis in very many American males.

Masculinity in America

This phenomenon of homosexual dread is, as we have stated explicitly, more of a problem for males than it is for females. The reason this is so is that the prohibition against intimate feelings toward one's own sex is much stronger for the male than for the female in our society. Males are supposed to be independent, rugged; they are not supposed to show tenderness toward each other; and when the stereotype is pushed toward its logical conclusion, they are not even allowed to show too much tenderness toward women. One of the factors accounting for the problem of intimacy between homosexual males is that, to the extent to which they have incorporated this masculine stereotype, they have also identified with a fear of dependency, so that neither of them wishes to be dependent on another male. Both wish to take the dominant role in the relationship and this leads to no end of conflict in any kind of attempt to form a stable partnership. Women, on the other hand, are encouraged to take a dependent role and so their egos are not threatened by becoming emotionally dependent on another person. This makes it much easier for them to form stable, enduring kinds of intimate associations with another member of the same sex.

Associated with the American concept of masculinity is the age-old degradation of women in Western society. It is not really necessary for me to review the history of the role of women in our society, since this has been done in innumerable books, but let me only remind the reader that Western women have always played, and still continue to play, the role of second-class citizens. In general, neither church nor state has admitted them to the highest position of honor, nor are they even allowed to enter into certain professions connected with the church. In our own country, it was only fairly recently that women were even allowed to vote in public elections. They have traditionally been relegated to the home, and assigned the role of mother and housekeeper. The crucial fact here is not that women have been assigned the role of rearing children, for this is not an unsuitable role for one who is physiologically capable of nursing the baby (although this role is not true for all known cultures). What *is* crucial is that this role has been considered a second-class role and that all the status and power in society have been given to males.

To a profound degree, masculinity is something which is more highly prized in our society than is femininity. Since it is more highly prized, it has to be achieved rather than simply taken for granted. Thus, in crucial aspects, it is harder to be accepted as a man than as a woman in American society. If this is so, then we can assume that this difficulty is not overcome by a number of individuals and that their feelings about their own masculinity are sufficiently vulnerable that they are subject to a number of problems, a few of which include (a) overt homosexuality, (b) schizophrenic breaks when homosexual feelings come to the surface, (c) a general sense of insecurity which is pervasive throughout the life of the individual, and (d) a compensatory Don Juan complex, in which the individual continually tries to prove that he is a man by seducing females.

Transsexualism

Transsexuals are members of one sex who wish to change and become members of the other sex. Most are males who wish to become females. They want to receive female hormones so that they will develop breasts and other female characteristics, such as a redistribution of body fat. And they wish sex-reassignment surgery so that the penis can be removed and an artificial vagina constructed. Some American medical centers are beginning to think that this is the best way to treat these men, as it is quite clear that they cannot be changed by psychotherapy. The evidence from psychological studies is that this incongruous gender role is fixed very early and is not amenable to traditional psychiatric treatment. The whole subject of transsexualism is a very complicated one, and while it is often confused in the public mind with homosexuality, it is really another variety of sexual deviation. Nevertheless, I am discussing it here because there is a crucial connection between the two phenomena which illuminates our general discussion in this chapter.

There is very good evidence from psychiatric studies of

transsexuals that some of them are transsexuals at least in part because they cannot bear the idea of being homosexual. They are actually males who wish sexual relations with other males. But they deny emphatically that they are homosexual. They say they aren't gay because they are not *really* males at all. They describe themselves as "females trapped in a male body," and they wish to escape from that body by having it altered so that it can be like a female one, i.e., with breasts, a vagina, no penis, etc. In this way they can get around the dread of homosexuality, because if a man who wishes to have sexual relations with another man *becomes a woman* he is no longer homosexual. He becomes, instead, a heterosexual woman. This is indeed a complex and difficult way around our cultural prohibition of homosexuality, but it "works," in a certain strange sense.

I do not wish to suggest that this is the principal dynamic involved in the development of most transsexuals, but it is an important factor and one which throws additional light on the manner in which our society creates psychopathology and the most tragic kinds of unhappiness by its current attitude toward homosexuality.

Mental Illness among Homosexuals

As we have pointed out, if one is not young and attractive, the gay world can be a very unhappy place indeed, for it has a very pervasive marketplace character. If one enters a market with very little to offer to the buyers to whom he desperately wishes to sell, then various serious personal troubles are likely to ensue, for one's self-esteem is constantly being deflated. Since the homosexual is viewed as a commodity in large parts of the gay world and judged by his cosmetic qualities, he soon begins to develop that same view of himself which is reflected back from other people. If he is viewed as a commodity of low value on the sexual market, he will begin to view himself as of little worth. This is, for many men, the beginning of mental illness of the most serious kind. There are, regrettably, no quantitative data on the matter, but it is my distinct impression that the homosexual world produces clinical depressions at a far higher rate than the heterosexual world, and though I cannot substantiate my opinion, I would venture to say that the suicide rate among male homosexuals is higher than among heterosexuals. This is of course not difficult to understand, in light of our analysis of the marketplace character of the gay world. Constant rejection from others produces a low opinion of one's own worth. Trying to play a game when one does not have the necessary attributes can only lead to very serious psychological troubles.

Obviously, the difficulty that homosexual men have in establishing intimate, lasting relationships is itself closely connected with the marketplace character of gay life and with the tendency for mental illness to occur among them. Especially as they become older, they find themselves increasingly less able to focus their lives around the seductive socializing that sustained them when they were younger. They become lonely and depressed and sometimes, at this age, first seek psychiatric advice. Not infrequently, they are able to establish a heterosexual marriage and rear a family. More often, they immerse themselves in their work and/or hobbies. If they can afford it, they may seek sex and a certain amount of (shallow) companionship from hustlers; this may be sexually satisfactory, but it does little to shore up the homosexual's self-esteem, since he knows that without the cold cash he would be alone.

There is a kind of chicken-and-egg paradox about the problem of promiscuity in the gay world. The very existence of the gay world is of course a product of social repression, just as the existence of an ethnic ghetto is the product of an analogous kind of repression. And yet, when one is in the world, one is subject to the mores and customs of that world, so that the promiscuity, which arises largely from the guilt about homosexuality which pervades our society, is itself reinforced by the gay world as a community. One hears homosexuals talk about gay marriages as if they were desirable, and one knows that these men are very often lonely and longing for some kind of permanence in their relationships with other males. Yet, at the same time, there is a premium placed on going to bed with a lot of attractive males, and on the kind of carefree playing around that the gay world tends to promote. One cannot, in analyzing the promiscuity of the gay world, leave out of account the influence which *it* plays in promoting this kind of interpersonal instability.

Nevertheless, what I have called sex fetishism is itself a direct result of the prohibition placed on homosexuality by the society. Sex fetishism involves an inordinate degree of emotional investment by the homosexual male focused around the problem of his sexuality. But it is clear, is it not, that this is a direct result of having his sexual feelings *defined as a problem* by the larger society in which he lives? In other words, the homosexual is forced into an excessive concentration on sexuality because his sexual feelings have been made an issue for him by his society. Thus, sex fetishism in the gay world is the logical product of the oppression to which the homosexual is subject by the very fact of his homosexuality.

So much of what goes on in the gay world can be understood if we see the homosexual community as a minority group subject to the same kinds of problems which other minority groups experience. Negroes are much more concerned with their skin color than are whites. The reason for this is obvious, namely, that their skin color has been defined as a problem by the larger society. In an analogous way, homosexuals are much more concerned with their sexuality than are heterosexuals, for the same reason, namely, that their sexual feelings have been defined as a problem by the straight world, and they have been subject to sanctions which are not altogether dissimilar from those which are thrust upon Negroes because of their skin color.

The gay world may thus be seen as a kind of non-geographical ghetto. It is not directly located on the map in clearly marked-off areas the way Negro and Mexican-American ghettos are, but it is a ghetto nevertheless and its inhabitants are subject to many of the same kinds of problems that other minority groups face. As Evelyn Hooker pointed out (1965b), there is a striking parallel between certain of the traits of minority group members who have been victimized by the larger society and many of the phenomena seen in the gay world. Hooker cites a number of "traits due to victimization" which are described by Gordon Allport in his book *The Nature of Prejudice* (1954) and says, "It would be strange indeed if all the traits caused by victimization in minority groups were, in the homosexual, produced by inner dynamics of the personality, for he too is a member of an out-group subject to extreme penalties, involving, according to Kinsey, 'cruelties [which] have not often been matched, except in religious and racial persecutions' (Kinsey, 1948, p. 17)" (Hooker, 1965b, p. 105).

As we have indicated before, many of the worst aspects of the gay world are caused by the need for anonymity which many of its members experience. One of the reasons why men make sexual contact in parks and lavatories is that this is one way of keeping their personal identity unknown to their sexual partner. Obviously, this kind of strategy is a direct result of the severe social sanctions which would ensue if the homosexual activities or orientation of the individual were known to members of his family, to his employers, and to the community at large.

The picture which emerges is that of the gay world as a bad scene, a bad scene produced by the attitude toward homosexuality on the part of the larger straight world, an attitude which itself is the result of the dread of homosexuality which pervades the culture and which goes hand in hand with repressed homosexual feelings on the part of millions in that culture. The price we pay for the luxury of allowing ourselves to believe that we have no erotic feelings toward members of our own sex is a very high price indeed. In this book I have tried to show how this price is paid by overt homosexuals, but in the present chapter I have also attempted to indicate that this price is paid for, very heavily, by individuals who are basically heterosexual. It is paid for in the form of severe mental illness, and in the form of a stereotyped concept of masculinity that frequently prevents males from having any warm, intimate feelings toward each other, even at a non-sexual level. This repression of tenderness between males is probably not unconnected, both historically and psychologically, with the training of men to be warriors, and thus may have something to do with the production of a state of mind in many of our citizens which has now become a positive danger to the perpetuation of our civilization.

Homosexuality and Alienation

I would like to close this chapter by connecting our analysis of homosexuality in America to a very suggestive paper by the sociologist Melvin Seeman (1959). According to Seeman, there are five basic ways in which the concept of alienation has been used. In my judgment, homosexuals are subject to alienating forces at all five of these levels. Seeman's first two categories define alienation as powerlessness and meaninglessness. He writes: "This variant of alienation can be conceived as *the expectancy or probability held by the individual that his own behavior cannot determine the occurrence of the outcomes, or reinforcements, he seeks*" (p. 784). And, in describing the second usage, Seeman writes, "it is characterized by a *low expectancy that satisfactory predictions about future outcomes of behavior can be made*" (p. 786). These are perfect descriptions of situations in which the homosexual is very often placed. He does not know what consequences his sexual orientation will have for him. He does not know what to expect from his family, from his employers, from his friends; he does not know what the gay world will be like when he goes into it; he has no cues from the mass media (such as the heterosexual does) on how he is to operate. When he does act, he cannot predict what kinds of outcomes will occur; in short, he is simply at the mercy of a host of chance factors.

Let me give two examples. If an individual picks up another man and takes him to his apartment, he really cannot predict what he is getting himself involved in. It may be a routine sexual encounter and, in fact, most often is. But it can also be a very disastrous encounter, because there are plenty of instances in which the individual has been beaten up, robbed, and sometimes murdered because he took a stranger home with him. If one reads between the lines in certain newspaper stories, one will very often find that some of the murders reported there have a homosexual theme. This does not mean, as it has sometimes been held, that homosexuals are unusually prone to violence. As we have indicated above, the reverse is true. It does mean, however, that homosexual men sometimes pick up either non-homosexuals who are out to rob them, or individuals who are sufficiently disturbed about their own sexual identity that, while they are able to go through with the sexual act, once they have consummated it, they are overcome by such a wave of guilt that the only way they can get rid of this is either to beat up or kill the partner. At an unconscious level, the beating or murder means to them that they have somehow absolved themselves of what they view as their sinful behavior.

A second example of the unpredictability involved in the gay world is that the homosexual cannot be sure what will happen when some organized institution becomes aware of his homosexuality. I have seen the entire gamut of reactions: from immediate dismissal of an individual on the slightest suspicion that he was homosexual, to individuals having been arrested and convicted for sexual behavior in public being kept on because of kindness and/or need for their services on the part of the organization to which they were attached.

These are of course but two examples, and the reader can surely think of many more areas in which there is simply no way of predicting what the outcome of disclosure will be. Certainly, homosexuals are very troubled about the reactions of their families, and while sometimes it is predictable that the family will be either accepting or completely hostile toward the homosexual son, in very many cases there is simply no way of knowing, and homosexuals go through all kinds of agony wondering whether or not they should let their parents know about their sexual orientation. Telling them, of course, runs the risk of ostracism, but not telling them very often means that the individual's feeling toward his family will undergo a marked change for the worse, for he will feel less close to a family to which he cannot disclose his closest feelings and his most serious problems. In a sense, he will, by *not* disclosing this information to the family, almost automatically suffer—although in a muted form—that distance he fears he will create by a frank disclosure.

Seeman's third category of alienation is normlessness, which is derived from the theorizing of the great French sociologist Emile Durkheim. Durkheim's description of anomie is of a condition in which social norms regulating individual conduct have broken down or are no longer effective as rules for behavior. Obviously, this meaning is closely connected with the first two meanings relating to control and prediction of future outcomes.

The homosexual is caught up in a world in which there are no guides for conduct. Homosexuality in America is an anomic situation. The individual doesn't know what to do; there are no structures of social rules to help govern his behavior. He is, as soon as his homosexuality becomes conscious to him, more or less cast adrift by society and left to fare on his own, with only the very unsatisfactory supports of the gay world to guide him in his actions. He is, of course, very often cast forth in a very tragic way by his family, his employers and his friends.

Society deals with homosexuality as if it did not exist. Although the situation is changing, this subject was not even discussed and was not even the object of scientific investigation until a few decades ago. We just didn't speak about these things; they were literally unspeakable and so loathsome that nothing could be said in polite society, or even in medical circles, about them. Aside from a few scientific books —many of them replete with stereotypes and inaccuracies— which were kept in special locked cabinets in the libraries of medical schools, individuals who had sensed in themselves the development of a homosexual orientation had nowhere to look for guidance. Physicians were untrained in this area because the subject was considered too unpleasant by all except psychiatry departments, which have, until recently, been held in low prestige by their medical colleagues. The whole treatment of homosexuals by the courts reflects, in many ways, a state of anomie, for the courts, as we have indicated in Chapter 5, very often act as if they wish they didn't have to be bothered by such unpleasant business as dealing with a homosexual arrest. In other words, society did not like the subject, did not want to discuss it, did not want to take intelligent social action toward it, did not want to help those afflicted with problems related to it. Society simply wanted to get rid of it, but it did not know how to do that.

We may note, in passing, what is undoubtedly the reason for the popularity of the disease concept of homosexuality, which we have attempted to show is a concept which is scientifically untenable. The reason for its popularity is simply that it offers a way out in conceptualizing the problem. People don't like to think of homosexuality as sinful any longer, because the whole concept of sin has gone out of Western culture. To describe homosexuality as morally evil is now unfashionable. And yet the alternative, considering it as a legitimate way of life for some people, is simply not palatable to very many. Hence, the popularity of the disease concept. If homosexuality is labeled an illness, we can avoid these other alternatives. We don't need to blame the homosexual, and yet we don't have to accept him. He is simply sick and hence what we really want to do is to find a way of curing him. A reading of Irving Bieber's book will make it very clear that its author implies that the problem of homosexuality can be solved by psychoanalytic treatment. This is so absurd a notion that I hesitate to take the reader's time to discuss it at any length. Is it really possible to conceive that a problem involving so many millions of men can be solved through individual treatment methods which were designed for an entirely different class of individuals, for neurotics, who felt a desire for a radical change in their life situation and who voluntarily sought psychiatric attention? When one looks at Bieber's colleagues' psychoanalyses, one finds that a great percentage of those who were persuaded to give up homosexuality were already bisexual in the first place, and that in order for this change to be effected, they typically had to undergo around 350 hours of psychoanalysis, which costs in the neighborhood of $10,000. If this were a logical solution to the homosexual problem, we might begin to ask the question whether it is a feasible solution in terms of (a) time, (b) personnel available, and (c) money available. But we don't even need to do this because the solution itself is not even reasonable, simply because most male homosexuals do not want to change their sexual orientation and will certainly not visit a psychoanalyst for the purpose of undergoing "treatment" for a sexual orientation that they don't want to alter. Hence the implied promise (of a general solution to the problem through psychotherapy) made by those psychiatrists who wish to define homosexuality as a disease makes absolutely no sense in any terms. It is not practical in any way, and its only real function is to permit us to avoid seeing the problem in its real light. Are we going to move toward a rational examination of this serious social problem, or are we going to continue, ostrich-like, with our heads in the sand and avoid thinking about what a rational solution to this problem would entail?

Seeman's fourth and fifth categories of alienation are isolation and self-estrangement. Throughout the book, and especially in the preceding chapter, I have tried to indicate the homosexual's isolation from his society as a whole, and his isolation or estrangement from himself. Society rejects him and he, following this lead, rejects himself, his own sexual orientation, and in so doing, rejects himself as a person and precludes the possibility of any kind of meaningful relationship with another man. This tragic situation is due, in large measure, to the view of homosexuality which is prevalent in the larger society. Pressures exist, both external (such as a need for anonymity on the part of many men who would be socially vulnerable if their sexual orientation were known) and internal (the self-denigration and concomitant denigration of the partner), that promote sex which is isolated from the rest of these men's lives. This is alienation of the most terrible kind, for it tends to fragment the existence of the homosexual, and dreprive him of the possibility—which heterosexuals take for granted—of integrating sex with love, and of working toward a development of the self and a structuring of one's life which would lead to a whole, rich involvement with another person.

EPILOGUE

○
● ●

What Is to Be Done?

As I indicated in the Introduction, a compelling scientific analysis of any serious social problem will carry with it implications for social change. If my analysis of the problem of homosexuality has been meaningful and convincing to the reader, he will at once see what needs to be done. Society as a whole must significantly shift its attitudes toward homosexuals and homosexuality in American life.

At one time in the history of our civilization, it was thought that unless everyone adhered to the same set of religious beliefs, society would crumble. The attempt to enforce religious

rmity upon the populace brought out the worst in man's
ͱ—including torture, war, and famine—and led to some
of the darkest pages in the history of man's treatment of his
fellow human creatures. Finally, at least in the contemporary
West, we have emerged from this abominable state of coer-
cion, and the history of the origins of America is, in part, a
history of the development of religious tolerance. Religious
tolerance means that we accept the idea that a society does
not require, in order for it to continue in existence, the suppression of world views and conceptions of reality other than
those held by the individuals who control power in the state.
The separation of church and state, which is written into our
Constitution, means that there exists for every citizen a private
sphere in which he can think for himself about religious matters and worship God in the way he wants—or not worship
at all, for that matter. This private sphere is guaranteed to
him by the state itself, which has been shown to be a quite
viable institution even without a uniform state religion.

What I am saying now is that the best solution to the
problem of homosexuality is one which is modeled on the
solution to the problem of religious difference, namely, a
radical tolerance for homosexual object-choice, whether as a
segment of an individual's sexual existence or as a full commitment to homosexuality as a way of life.

I suggest that we view homosexuals as a minority group,
and begin to seriously consider giving them the full legal
rights and social privileges that we *have* finally given to some
minority groups (e.g., Roman Catholics) and that we talk
about giving to others. This means, among other things, we
will have to: (1) abolish the penalties that now exist for
certain kinds of sexual relations between consenting adults
in private; (2) end police activity against homosexuals, in
all its forms, including use of decoys and harassment of gay

bars and other homosexual meeting places; (3) cease firing government employees (including members of the armed forces) because they are thought to be homosexual; (4) encourage private industry to cease similar treatment of homosexual employees.

Homosexual sexual activity should be subject to no more stringent regulation than heterosexual activity. If, and only if, it becomes a genuine annoyance to those who do not wish involvement should the activity be subject to legal sanction. For example, if non-homosexual men are frequently annoyed by promiscuous homosexuals in certain lavatories, it would be appropriate for the police to guarantee these non-homosexuals their right to use these facilities in peace and quiet. There is, however, absolutely no moral justification for the harassment of gay bars and baths by police agencies and the arrest of respectable citizens in such locales. As a matter of fact, such establishments should be allowed to publicly advertise and label themselves as catering to homosexuals. They should, in other words, be allowed to exist officially, so that homosexuals may feel less ashamed about going into these places, and also so that heterosexuals may know beforehand to what kind of clientele they cater.

These specific changes would, to a large degree, need to be predicated upon and be associated with a real change in the overall public attitude toward homosexuality. Instead of viewing this form of object-choice as an unspeakable horror, or even as a mental disease, the public should be encouraged to see it as what it actually is, i.e., a variation in the sexual impulse, which is one of the possible outcomes of human sexual development, and—most significantly—one which need not do harm to anyone. If the social attitude could move in this direction, we would see the causal connection between homosexuality and psychopathology—which now exists in certain forms, as I have indicated in preceding chapters—begin to recede. We would see homosexuals develop into better-adjusted persons and we would, in my judgment, see less sex fetishism and instability of relationships in the gay world.

To carry this analysis to its utopian conclusion, we would see the end of the gay world as a hidden, deviant subculture, lurking in the unhappy interstices of the larger society. Instead, we would simply see homosexuals and heterosexuals and bisexuals within our social world, all living their lives without having to endure persecution.

Is this all a utopian dream? Is it really possible? Frankly, I don't know. Our society, like most others, is very slow in changing social attitudes, especially ones which go as deep into the hearts of the populace as do feelings about sexuality. Still, changes *are* occurring. During the past decade both England and Illinois have abolished age-old statutes prohibiting homosexual men from having sexual relations in private. While such legal changes are only a beginning, they *are* a necessary beginning, and they do indicate a greater degree of tolerance in the society as a whole.

There are other encouraging signs. Homosexuality is now being discussed in popular magazines, on television, in the sex education courses that are developing in our schools. Many are discovering that homosexuals are real people, not rare oddities of fun, and that perhaps they should be treated with human dignity.

I cannot say where this will lead or how soon (if ever) the changes I advocate will occur. Most of what I can do to help I have already done, here in this volume.

References

Allport, Gordon W. (1954). *The Nature of Prejudice*. Cambridge, Mass.: Addison Wesley.

Baldwin, James (1956). *Giovanni's Room*. New York: Dial Press.

Beach, Frank A., ed. (1965). *Sex and Behavior*. New York: Wiley.

Becker, Ernest (1964). *The Revolution in Psychiatry*. New York: The Free Press of Glencoe.

Bieber, Irving, *et al.* (1962). *Homosexuality*. New York: Basic Books.

Bowlby, John (1961). "Separation Anxiety: A Critical Review of the Literature," *Journal of Child Psychology and Psychiatry*, I, 251.

Cavan, Sherri (1966). *Liquor License: An Ethnography of Bar Behavior*. Chicago: Aldine.

Collingwood, R. G. (1960). *The Idea of Nature*. New York: Galaxy Books.

Crombie, A. C. (1959). *Medieval and Early Modern Science*. Garden City, N.Y.: Doubleday Anchor Books.

Curran, Desmond, and Parr, Denis (1957). "Homosexuality: An Analysis of 100 Male Cases Seen in Private Practice," *British Medical Journal*, April 6, 1957, pp. 797–801.

Dewey, John (1910). *The Influence of Darwinism on Philosophy and Other Essays in Contemporary Thought*. New York: Holt.

Fenichel, Otto (1945). *The Psychoanalytic Theory of Neurosis*. New York: Norton.

Freud, Sigmund (1911). *Psycho-analytic Notes upon an Autobiographical Account of a Case of Paranoia (Dementia Paranoides)*. Strachey translation. In *Collected Papers*, Vol. III. New York: Basic Books (1959).

Freud, Sigmund (1925). *Three Essays on the Theory of Sexuality*. Strachey translation. New York: Basic Books (1962).

Freud, Sigmund (1930). *Civilization and Its Discontents*. Riviere translation. London: Hogarth Press.

Gebhard, Paul, Gagnon, John, Pomeroy, Wardell, and Christenson, Cornelia (1965). *Sex Offenders*. New York: Harper-Hoeber.

Green, Richard, and Money, John (1966). "Stage-Acting, Role-Taking, and Effeminate Impersonation during Boyhood," A.M.A. *Archives of General Psychiatry*, XV, 535.

Hampson, John L. (1965). "Determinants of Psychosexual Orientation," in Beach (1965).

Harlow, Harry F. (1962). "The Heterosexual Affectional System in Monkeys," *American Psychologist*, January, 1962.

Hoffman, Martin (1964). "Drug Addiction and 'Hypersexuality': Related Modes of Mastery," *Comprehensive Psychiatry*, V, 262.

Hoffman, Martin (1966). Review of Schofield (1965), in *Issues in Criminology*, II, 313.

Hooker, Evelyn (1957). "The Adjustment of the Male Overt Homosexual," *Journal of Projective Techniques*, XXI, 18.

Hooker, Evelyn (1965a). "An Empirical Study of Some Relations between Sexual Patterns and Gender Identity in Male Homosexuals," in John Money, ed., *Sex Research: New Developments*. New York: Holt, Rinehart and Winston.

Hooker, Evelyn (1965b). "Male Homosexuals and Their 'Worlds'," in Judd Marmor, ed., *Sexual Inversion*. New York: Basic Books.

Keniston, Kenneth (1965). *The Uncommitted: Alienated Youth in American Society*. New York: Harcourt, Brace and World.

Kinsey, Alfred, Pomeroy, Wardell, and Martin, Clyde (1948). *Sexual Behavior in the Human Male*. Philadelphia: W. B. Saunders.

Kinsey, Alfred, Pomeroy, Wardell, Martin, Clyde, and Gebhard, Paul (1953). *Sexual Behavior in the Human Female*. Philadelphia: W. B. Saunders.

Laswell, Harold D. (1962). *Power and Personality*. New York: Compass Books.

Money, John, Hampson, Joan G., and Hampson, John L. (1955). "An Examination of Some Basic Sexual Concepts: The Evidence of Human Hermaphroditism," *Bulletin of the Johns Hopkins Hospital*, XCVII, 301.

Murray, Gilbert (1951). *Five Stages of Greek Religion*. Boston: Beacon Press.

Nagel, Ernest (1961). *The Structure of Science: Problems in the Logic of Scientific Explanation*. New York: Harcourt, Brace and World.

Parsons, Talcott (1954). *The Incest Taboo in Relation to Social Structure and the Socialization of the Child*. Reprinted in *Social*

Structure and Personality (1964). New York: Free Press of Glencoe.
Ploscoe, Morris (1962). *Sex and the Law.* New York: Ace Books.
Rado, Sandor (1940). "A Critical Examination of the Concept of Bisexuality," *Psychosomatic Medicine,* II, 459.
Rechy, John (1963). *City of Night.* New York: Grove Press.
Rechy, John (1967). *Numbers.* New York: Grove Press.
Schofield, Michael (1965). *Sociological Aspects of Homosexuality.* London: Longmans.
Seeman, Melvin (1959). "On the Meaning of Alienation," *American Sociological Review,* XXIV, 783.
Stearn, Jess (1961). *The Sixth Man.* Garden City, N.Y.: Doubleday.
Stoller, Robert J. (1965). "The Sense of Maleness," *Psychoanalytic Quarterly,* XXXIV, 207.
Sullivan, Harry Stack (1953). *The Interpersonal Theory of Psychiatry.* New York: Norton.
van den Haag, Ernest (1963). "Notes on Homosexuality and Its Cultural Setting," in H. M. Ruitenbeek, ed., *The Problem of Homosexuality in Modern Society.* New York: E. P. Dutton.
Wild, John (1953). *Plato's Modern Enemies and the Theory of Natural Law.* Chicago: University of Chicago Press.

Index

acting, interest in, 22, 24, 25, 72–74
adolescent heterosexual play, 20
adolescent homosexual play, 20, 25
adolescent peer relationships, 119, 123, 133, 135, 150–151
after-bar parties, 76–77
after-hours coffee houses, 76
alienation, homosexuality and, 152–153, 192–198
all-Negro gay bars, 71–72
Allport, Gordon, 191
American Law Institute, 95, 96, 98; Model Penal Code, 95, 98–99
anal intercourse, 19, 25, 36–38, 40, 41, 50, 61, 74, 77, 143, 146; and children, 93; law and, 80–82, 88, 90, 91, 106, 112; among married couples, 81, 106, 112
animism, primitive forms of, 104
anomie, 115, 195, 196
anonymity, homosexuality and, 17, 23, 51, 59, 179, 191, 198
anxiety: avoidance of, 117, 118; castration, 144–147, 165; childhood, 117, 118; and mental illness, 121; primary genital, 126–127
anxiety states, 184
Aristotelian philosophy, 102–108, 110, 111
arrests, homosexual, 48, 82–89, 97–98, 194, 196, 201
arts, interest in, 22, 24, 25, 72–74
asexual relations, 67–68

Bacon, Francis, 108
bar-hopping, 12, 23

bars: arrests in, 87; gay, 9, 11–12, 15–18, 21, 22, 26–28, 34, 44, 49, 53–61, 71–72; lesbian, 54, 167
baths, homosexual, 18, 21, 22, 44, 48–52, 59–60, 76, 77; arrests in, 87
Beach, Frank, 124, 125, 128, 135–136
beaches, contacts on, 18, 21; arrests for, 87
Becker, Ernest, 121
Biblical prohibition against homosexuality, 100
Bieber, Irving, 38, 39, 122, 123, 147–148, 150, 156–159, 161, 164, 165, 173, 196–197
bisexuality, 15–24, 31–32, 50–52, 94, 152, 197, 202; constitutional, 121, 122, 149, 150, 184; Freudian concept of, 121, 123, 149, 184
bohemian life-style, 153
Bowlby, John, 117
Brahe, Tycho, 108, 109
British Medical Journal, 160
buggery, 100

California Penal Code, 81–82, 84
castration anxiety, 144–147, 165
Cavan, Sherri, 57
Chicago, homosexuals in, 26, 79, 97–98
child-parent interactions, 116–120, 123–127, 133, 135–137, 146–149
childhood anxiety, 117, 118
children, homosexual crimes against, 92–95

206